The Making of a Music Academy

Jerome Stanley

Hamilton Books

An Imprint of
Rowman & Littlefield
Lanham • Boulder • New York • Toronto • Plymouth, UK

Copyright © 2016 by Hamilton Books
4501 Forbes Boulevard, Suite 200, Lanham, Maryland 20706
Hamilton Books Acquisitions Department (301) 459-3366

Unit A, Whitacre Mews, 26-34 Stannary Street,
London SE11 4AB, United Kingdom

All rights reserved
Printed in the United States of America
British Library Cataloguing in Publication Information Available

Library of Congress Control Number: 2015950244
ISBN: 978-0-7618-6666-4 (pbk : alk. paper)—ISBN: 978-0-7618-6667-1 (electronic)

Cover photograph: Miami University musicians at Carnegie Hall, New York. Photo by Jeff Sabo, Miami University

∞™ The paper used in this publication meets the minimum requirements of American National Standard for Information Sciences Permanence of Paper for Printed Library Materials, ANSI/NISO Z39.48-1992.

The soul is composed of harmony
—Leonardo da Vinci

Contents

Note to the Reader		vii
Foreword		ix
Introduction		xi
1	Beginnings	1
2	Laying the Foundations: 1900–1920	7
3	Leadership and Music Organizations: 1920s	13
4	A Decade of Growth: 1930s	19
5	Further Expansion of the Department: 1940s	27
6	Oxford String Quartet	33
7	A Half-Century of Achievement: 1950s	41
8	Merging of Two Faculties: 1960s	49
9	A New Physical Facility: 1970s	55
10	A Dynamic Period: 1980s	65
11	The New Century: 1990s and 2000s	75
12	Opera and Musicals at Miami	85
13	Music Faculty in Luxembourg and Echternach Festival Orchestra	91
14	Dreams Come True	97
15	University Artists Series and Department Residencies	107
16	The Larger Community	113
17	Conclusion and Future: Year of the Arts	117
Appendix A: Music Faculty as of October 2010		129

Appendix B: Non-tenured & Temporary Faculty: Part-time &
    Adjunct Faculty; and Branch Campus Faculty   133

Appendix C: Miami Opera Productions 1998–2012   137

Appendix D: Miami University Musicals 1980–2007   139

Appendix E: Interviews with Faculty and Graduates   141

Appendix F: Donors to the Building of the Center for Performing Arts 147

Appendix G: Music Scholarships & Awards   149

Appendix H: List of Interviewees   151

Appendix I: Credits   153

About the Author   155

Note to the Reader

The settlers of the New World brought with them the music from their homelands and built schools of music to insure the continuity of the art form. Miami University, today a coeducational research university located in Oxford, Ohio, in the United States, was among the early American institutions established in the western part of the new country. An act of the U.S. Congress, signed by President George Washington, set aside a tract of land in the southwestern corner of Ohio as the site for the building of a university. The university was formally chartered in 1809, although classes were not held until 1824. It is the 10th oldest public university in the United States and the second oldest university in Ohio, founded four years after Ohio University in Athens, Ohio.

In its 2012 edition, *U.S. News and World Report* ranked the university 3rd for best undergraduate teaching at national universities, and 90th in the overall rankings. Forbes also ranked Miami University as 34th among U.S. public universities and 1st among public universities within Ohio. Miami University has over 400 student-run organizations. Aside from the university's student newspaper, the university's oldest and longest-running student organization is the Miami University Men's Glee Club founded in 1907. It is estimated to be the 16th oldest Glee Club in the nation. The Department of Music in The School of Creative Arts began in the first years of the twentieth century and has grown to its present status as a nationally recognized Department with students from abroad as well as from across the United States.

This is a story about the building of a music program as an integral part of a liberal arts curriculum. It is a story that has been repeated at many educational institutions. It allows us to honor those who have given their talents and devoted their careers to teaching and preparation of the younger generations in music education. It is also an art survival story. Miami University always placed strong emphasis on sports, especially football. But music, which is also a highly competitive team effort, did not receive equal funding with sports. And yet, the determination of the music faculty brought accolades to the Department of Music.

To give equal space to all music faculty members at Miami University through the decades since 1902 is not the purpose of this book, but all faculty names found during the research are listed. It has been the author's purpose to pay tribute to full-time music faculty members who gave long years of service and were active in the governmental process of the Department of Music, as well as the building of the performance studios. The final year for inclusion of faculty members is 2010. Likewise, the Deans of the School of Fine Arts included here are those who were in that office for at least two years and demonstrated outstanding leadership. Acting Deans serving in a temporary capacity have not been included.

Two branch campuses of Miami University were established in the late 1960s. Music faculty members from the branch campuses are identified by name, without biographical information, in a separate appendix. The author has attempted to include the names of all music faculty in the history of the University up to the year 2010 and will appreciate notification of any inadvertent omissions.

The following Foreword was written by Dr. Everett F. Nelson, Chair of the Department of Music from 1951 to 1972. He contributed his comments in 2013 as he celebrated his 100th birthday.

Foreword

For many decades before my arrival, Music at Miami was a flourishing tradition. Miami music graduates were in charge of music programs around the State of Ohio as band, orchestra directors and also elementary music teachers. Also, numbers of them were serving as church organists and choir directors.

Irving Hamilton was my first student to graduate from Miami. He became the Music Supervisor of the Hamilton City Schools and also a life-long friend. Soon I met many other Miami music graduates around the state who were capable directors of instrumental and choral groups in their high schools. All of them were genuine Boosters of the Miami Music program. Certainly the Ohio high school students entering as freshman were often encouraged to do so by a former Miamian who was a music teacher. A much smaller group of entering students were from out-of-state and undoubtedly had heard of the first rate reputation of Miami's music program.

Attending concerts and performances at Miami gave me truly wonderful moments of fulfillment. There are too many of them to begin writing about in acknowledgement of my thanks to those who gave me such thrilling experiences. However, the concerts of the Beethoven 9th Symphony when the Miami Choruses joined the Cincinnati Symphony Orchestra and the Dayton Philharmonic Orchestra were especially moving for me.

As Chair of the Music Department, I was supported by a capable, well-trained and talented faculty dedicated to performing and teaching, as well as students who were eager to perform and teach music. As Chairperson, I tried to keep an encouraging control of the Music Department in which the generous and friendly faculty could successfully achieve their objectives. Clearly, it was a privilege and reward to spend my years at Miami with the music faculty and students. How well my tenure of several decades was successful is certainly revealed by remarks from faculty members and former students.

Through my years at Miami this situation remained a stable goal of the University Administration, so that new faculty members were approved whenever vacancies occurred in the faculty. When the new Theater-Music building was built, the Music Department added a Music Librarian and a piano technician to the staff plus part time member from the Cincinnati Symphony to teach flute, bassoon, string bass and trombone.

When I started at Miami University, the Music Education Department was on the third floor of McGuffey School then located in the south side of the School of Education building. The four available classrooms there were used by both the Music Education and Music Departments. The Music Department was located in a house on High Street plus in a wooden barracks left standing after the war. When the two Departments were combined as the Music Department in the School of Fine Arts, they were moved to Benton Hall that had been University Administration Offices. Also Hepburn Hall was acquired as an additional building for the Music Department.

Of course over the years I heard several rumors about shifts in the priorities of what new building would be next. Several times the Music Building was put lower on the list for different reasons. I never knew about this shifting of priorities as a part of my job. Certainly the Dean of Fine Arts kept pushing for a new building. After years of starts and stops, the University planning and building committee selected the Music-Theater building to be built.

Dr. Everett F. Nelson
Barrington, New Hampshire, 2013
Chair, Department of Music
1951–1972

Introduction

It is the author's hope that this book will, among other things, enlighten the reader concerning some of the difficulties that may be found in the efforts to advance the stature of music programs at our American educational institutions. It has been said that society tends, in general, to give a lower priority to music and the arts compared with other areas in the educational system. One has only to notice how, when there is a budget problem in education, art and music are the first subjects to be cut. The book is also intended to focus upon the achievements of music making at Miami University in Oxford, Ohio, through the decades from the late nineteenth century into the early twenty-first century.

The making of a quality music program at an institution of higher learning requires time, vision, dedication and energy. Any academy comes into being through the integrity and ingenuity of its creators. In view of this, it is fitting to pay homage to the individuals whose vision, time and energy have left a lasting legacy. The author wishes to give the reader an account of the highly trained and dedicated music faculty members of the Miami University Department of Music who have devoted their lives to the mission of educating the future musical leaders of society.

Discovery, intuition and inspiration are human experiences that are both individual and collective. These are at the very core of any community of students and faculty at a music school. This is an important point and one often missed by politicians and administrators whose work lies in different areas than the very acts of creation involved in music study and performance. The greatest success of an academy occurs when there is a mutual understanding of all parties involved.

This book celebrates the accomplishments of faculty and students who contributed to the excellence of the Department of Music at Miami University. It covers a period of over one hundred years including the music faculty members up to the year 2010. Every effort has been made to include the names of faculty and administrators of the Department during those years. The author apologizes for any inadvertent omissions. Students and faculty of the future may find inspiration through some knowledge of their predecessors. Too often we forget their struggles against political and financial obstacles. Fortunately for us, artists and musicians cling steadfastly to their conviction that art must survive in any civilized society.

The book also celebrates music itself and advocates the need to preserve 'classical music' of all cultures, a term that is easily misunderstood and allowed to languish in the education of the young. It must be learned that classical music in all cultures is not merely 'show' or 'entertainment,' but rather an expression of a deeper spiritual life.

Music has been the common language among people for thousands of years. We must begin by recognizing that the human race has an irresistible urge to create. This has been recorded in all human societies. Music is a language understood by all, irrespective of their native tongue and profession. At our universities, students from all of the various academic disciplines come together in a variety of musical organizations. Though they may be unable to explain to each other their individual academic pursuits, they communicate with each other through the common understanding of music.

In Western civilization alone, the lasting achievements in the arts speak of the creative impulse to record and preserve the beauty of the ages. This impulse is rooted in all of us and seeks to spread itself throughout all of society for the betterment of mankind. In an imperfect world, the creative arts in education allow students to experience both the joy and the discipline of working toward perfection of a personal artistic expression. Many studies have been done showing the value of music to the education of the young, based upon modern scientific research. One such source is Kristin Leutwyler's "Exploring the Musical Brain," in *Scientific American* (2009).

The Florida Music Educators Association makes the following statement about music education:

> Music and the Fine Arts have been a significant portion of every culture's educational system for more than 3,000 years. The human brain has been shown to be "hard-wired" for music; there is a biological basis for music being an important part of human experience. Music and the Arts surround daily life in our present day culture. Most present day artists, architects, and musicians acquired their interests during public school Fine Arts classes... Education without the Fine Arts is fundamentally impoverished and subsequently leads to an impoverished society.

America's cultural history originated from the European tradition, gradually assimilating influences from other traditions, and finally culminating in new art forms as our nation moved from the eighteenth to the twenty-first century. In classical music, the first American educational leaders were centered in the area of Boston, Massachusetts. They represented the importation of the highest standards of European music conservatories and the composers associated with them.

As the American population expanded westward from New England, there was an increasing demand for educational institutions in the Midwest and finally on the West Coast. In 1794, President George Washington signed a patent for government purchase of land in the rolling hills of southwestern Ohio that would eventually be the home of Miami University. Before the arrival of Europeans, the land had been the home of the Miami tribe of Native Americans. The new university was chartered in 1809, and the institution opened its doors to students in 1824. The charter year of 1809 was the same year in which the composer Franz Joseph Haydn died in his native Vienna while the city was being bombarded by Napoleon's army.

Miami University, at the time of its founding, was considered to be in the far western part of the nation, since the Mississippi River, for all practical purposes, marked the western-most boundary of the nation. The idea of its founders was to create a community with an educational environment similar to that found in England, where several colleges were gathered together. This is probably the reason why the town that grew alongside Miami University was named Oxford. The founding fathers of the university chose a rural setting that they felt would be ideal for the new university.

Co-educational institutions did not yet exist in America. Women were educated in separate colleges. Therefore, Miami University was at one time surrounded by several different women's colleges, one of which was named The Western College for Women (founded in 1853), its location being considered in the far west of the country at the time. Although it is the author's intent to deal in this book with Miami University's Department of Music, it is necessary to include some discussion of the Music Department at The Western College for Women and its contribution to the community of musical scholars and performers. As will be seen, the Oxford community comprised a unique era of creativity.

The strictly classical curriculum of nineteenth-century Miami University did not include music and the arts. However, by the end of the century the institution boasted a band of musicians known as the Mandolin Club. Eventually, in the very earliest years of the twentieth century, student musical organizations began to appear. A small orchestra was formed as well as choral groups. The original classic curriculum eventually transformed naturally into the liberal arts concept of education, and soon a Department of Music would be part of this tradition.

After World War I, the University established the School of Fine Arts that included the Departments of Art, Architecture and Music. Later, the Theatre

Department and a small dance program were added to the School. These departments were housed in separate quarters for several decades until 1969, with the various classes and activities of the music department being scattered among four different buildings quite remote from one another.

With the opening of the Center for Performing Arts in 1969, a new chapter opened for the Department of Music. For the first time, there was a recital hall with 150 seats. The plans for the building called for a large auditorium adjacent to the Center that would have been an ideal space for large concerts featuring the large ensembles such as the opera, orchestra, concert band, and various choral groups. Unfortunately, this facility was never built. The result was that the large organizations had to continue using a hall at the opposite end of the campus that was built in 1910 and now known as Hall Auditorium. It was renovated during 1991 to 1993 to better accommodate the Department's needs, but its campus location made it problematic for various reasons.

The twentieth century saw the Department of Music grow from its inception, over a period of eighty years, into a widely respected undergraduate school with students from abroad as well as from many different regions of the United States. The year 2012 was proclaimed as 'The Year of the Arts' at Miami University, and the School of Fine Arts was renamed The School of Creative Arts.

A gala concert in New York's Carnegie Hall featuring student and faculty musicians celebrated The Year of the Arts on October 7, 2012. It was a fitting tribute to the decades of leadership and faculty devotion to the goal of providing the highest standard of music education at Miami University.

Jerome Stanley
Oxford, Ohio
March, 2013

Chapter One

Beginnings

For centuries, the human race has passed along its stories to the younger generations. Through storytelling we gain glimpses of our civilization that otherwise would go unnoticed. Societies value storytelling and the study of history as a means for continually evaluating the past in order to inform and instruct the present and the future. Without history, we are the blind leading the blind. In some ways, the past seems even more concrete than the present. We can look to it as a blueprint for guidance.

In the European tradition, the centuries-old system of studying music was by way of apprenticeship in which a student was under the tutelage of a master. The Renaissance saw the appearance of a number of music conservatories staffed by professional musicians. Within these institutions the system of one-on-one pedagogical training continued. This system has endured to the present day as the primary means of music performance training.

The concept of the music conservatory was brought to the United States by the European immigrants. The first American conservatories appeared in New England. Gradually the concept spread to other regions of the country. These institutions were separate from colleges and universities, but over time these independent conservatories merged with the academic institutions, often for financial reasons.

One might imagine that the beginnings of music at Miami were to be found in special musical offerings on an occasional basis, as well as in small extracurricular volunteer groups. The Miami University Archives possesses some printed concert programs from the 1880s and 1890s, documenting performances of piano, violin and cello, as well as a group called the Miami University Minstrels. A volunteer group from the 1890s was called the Mandolin Club, which could consist of various instruments other than mandolins. This photograph, circa 1890, shows the Club comprised of seven musicians only one of which holds a mandolin, the others being guitars and banjos. Other photos of the Mandolin Club located in the Miami University Archives reveal how the instrumentation could vary in different years. One year the group has two mandolins, two guitars, a flute and a large bowed string instrument that appears to be a cello. . The Mandolin Club of 1906 consisted of mandolins, guitars and banjos.

Records indicate that in 1902 the University employed an instructor of music, A. J. Gantvoort, whose previous position was business manager of the College of Music of Cincinnati. By 1906 a Music Department had been established in the College of Liberal Arts, including instruction in harmony, composition and the history of music.

By 1915 the Department of Music included two choral groups, one called The Arion Choir and the other the Madrigal Club. An Archive program from 1921 announces the "First May Musical Festival at Oxford, Ohio." Presumably, the name of this festival might have been inspired by the well-established May Festival in Cincinnati. Oxford's May Festival in 1921 included four concerts in three days, with Aubrey W. Martin as Musical Director, and

The Mandolin Club, 1906. Image provided by Miami University Libraries, Oxford, OH.

offered major works by European composers and Miami's own composer, Joseph Clokey.

MIAMI UNIVERSITY ORCHESTRA HISTORY

The 1906 Department was headed by Dr. Shilo Shaffer Myers, who also directed the Miami University Orchestra. In 1905, the orchestra consisted of sixteen men. Two years later, fourteen men and three women comprised the orchestra's membership.

Musical organizations on campus then consisted of an orchestra, a large mixed chorus of forty-six women and twenty-three men, a ladies' glee club of thirteen women, a men's glee club of ten men, and a mandolin club of six or seven men. The presence of these groups on campus undoubtedly enhanced the spirit of the student body and the community at large.

The Miami University Orchestra dates back as far as 1890 to the Miami Stringed Orchestra, which consisted entirely of banjos, mandolin, guitars, and piccolo-banjos. It was not until 1903, however, that the Miami University Symphony Orchestra was officially founded. At its inception, this twelve-member ensemble, under the direction of Dr. S. S. Myers, served to play each morning in the university chapel service and at most university functions. An article in the December 1904 edition of The Miami Student reads in part, ". . . since its organization a year ago, [the Miami orchestra] has perhaps contributed more to the pleasure of the college life of Miami than any other organization . . ." An editorial in the January 1905 Miami Student later boasts, "Both students and faculties can feel justly proud of our Orchestra. It is a living exemplification of the precept, that whatever is worth doing at all, is worth doing well . . . it would not be an exaggeration to say that it is the flower of the music department."

Miami University Orchestra, 1905. Image provided by Miami University Libraries, Oxford, OH.

The University Orchestra was already making regional tours under the direction of Dr. Myers. An article in the *Miami Student* newspaper issue of April, 1905, describes the orchestra tours for March of that year:

> On Monday evening, March twenty-seventh, the Miami University Orchestra gave a concert at Sidney, Ohio . . . The goodly attendance was, no doubt, due in part to the fact that Dr. S. S. Myers had charge of the music in the Sidney Public Schools before he came to Miami . . . On Tuesday evening, March twenty-eighth, the orchestra gave a concert at Dayton, Ohio . . . Those who attended the concert expecting to listen to an ordinary band of college musicians were agreeably surprised.

Soon after 1905, however, the orchestra was forced to disband as the number of instrumentalists at the university dwindled. Ten years later, in 1915, plans to revive the orchestra were undertaken. The Miami Student announced on November 25, 1915, "The development of the university orchestra is well under way, for the most difficult part of the process—that of securing the talent was easily accomplished." The premiere of this new ensemble took place on December 15, 1916, in the First Concert of the Miami University Orchestra with a 44-member ensemble held in Benton Hall (now Hall Auditorium) under the direction of noted composer and conductor Joseph W. Clokey.

In April of 1908, the newspaper reports the performance of a music program in the Miami Chapel on March 8th. On the program were singers, pianists and the Orchestra. Some of the more familiar composers represented on the program were Beethoven (Sonata, Op. 28), Franz Abt, Mascagni and Schubert.

Over the next several decades, the orchestra's leadership included conductors Donald Kissane, Roy A. Williams, Lloyd Outland, Dr. Theodore Kratt, Gordon Sutherland, Joseph Bein, Adon Foster and George Seltzer. In 1957, the university secured conductor and composer Otto Frohlich, a native of Czechoslovakia, to direct the orchestra and the newly organized student opera program. Frohlich's twelve-year tenure with the orchestra contributed a great deal to the success of both the ensemble and the music department.

After Frohlich's retirement, the ensemble was directed by George Seltzer and later Paul Nadler. Carmon DeLeone, director of the acclaimed Cincinnati Ballet, served as director of the orchestra from 1980-1992. Following DeLeone were conductors Gary A. Speck, Jacob Chi and Jose-Luis Novo who, in 1998, founded the Oxford Chamber Orchestra out of a collaboration between music faculty and select students. According to Novo, "The main goal of this orchestra is to provide real-life performance situations for students with the sort of musical interaction with their teachers that cannot be duplicated in the studio setting." Following Novo was interim conductor Jaime Morales-Matos. In the fall of 2002, Ricardo Averbach, a native of Brazil, was appointed as conductor of the Miami University Symphony Orchestra, a position that he still occupied in 2013.

NEW ENSEMBLES APPEAR

In the October, 1908, edition of *The Miami Student* there appeared notices of music organizations in progress:

> Through the efforts of Professor Burke, a ladies' chorus has been organized, consisting of twenty-one young ladies of the University. This organization is known as the Madrigal Club.
>
> The Glee Club is now entering on the second year of its existence . . . At the home concert, the first appearance of the club, the audience was surprised, for it never dreamed that, lurking in the men of "Old Miami," was such talent, such harmony, or such power of entertainment by song.
>
> The response to the call for the organization of a University band was most gratifying, and exceeded the expectations of those most deeply interested. Seventeen men reported, and an organization was effected, Solon J. Carter being selected leader.

POST WORLD WAR I

After World War I, the nation was able to resume a peacetime environment. Part of this new environment was shaped by a change in the nation's musical fabric. Now, the Old World musical influence became juxtaposed to the newer American elements including ragtime and jazz. At first, these old and new styles seemed to have been somewhat like oil and water – they performed different roles in society and did not mix together. But under the surface, and at the hands of the young generation of American composers, the two styles began to coalesce.

It was just at this period when the School of Fine Arts was established at Miami University. The young George Gershwin was at the height of his powers, bringing to the American public a new brand of music that joined the old with the new. By 1929 he and his brother Ira had already produced several Broadway musicals and a one-act opera. America's youth were growing up listening to radio and phonograph recordings of jazz and other popular music, but it would be some time before jazz music would be introduced into the curriculum of American universities.

Here we pause for some reflection upon possible reasons why European classical music was the only type of music sanctioned by the early conservatories and university programs. It can be argued that classical music probes deeply into human experience in a similar way that classical literature does. During the eighteenth and nineteenth centuries, a strong European pedagogical system was in place emphasizing a connection between classical literature and music. One must say that this emphasis is still today an interest among composers of concert hall music.

At the same time, a new American outlook on music began to emerge through the works of the young generation of composers in the early twentieth century. This eventually led to an attitude by the end of that century in which some critics began to speak of European classical music as being that of 'dead white men.' The trend was now toward re-defining music in a way that moved further away from the strictly older European ideal of placing music within the 'world of ideas' connected with classical literature. The new trend viewed music as very much a 'now' aesthetic. Thus, non-current older forms of music became categorized as 'historical music.' At the same time, the new age of music education became aware of the need to recognize global music.

What were once independent conservatories have now merged with universities. They continue to follow the apprenticeship model for performance pedagogy, and student demand for this model is continuing at a high level. But meanwhile, universities throughout the country developed their own schools and departments of music within a humanities or fine arts context. The faculties of these institutions have faced the huge challenge of developing meaningful curricula that provide a balance between the traditional and contemporary art forms. Modern music education must deal with the temptation to throw out the baby with the bathwater. It is probably an old but wise statement that reducing musical studies of the European classics in a music curriculum would be like reducing studies of Shakespeare's works in an English program to allow more time for modern works.

Chapter Two

Laying the Foundations

1900–1920

An annual series of musical and lecture programs existed at Miami University as early as 1899. It was called The Union Lyceum Course. This series eventually evolved into the Miami University Artists Series. For the 1899-1900 season, we notice the inclusion of European composers Edvard Grieg and others, in addition to the then contemporary American composer Edward MacDowell.

With the advent of President Benton the University began to add cultural features, extra curricular, consisting chiefly of lectures, public addresses and musical programs. These programs were for the benefit of the three separate colleges in Oxford at the time: Miami University, Western College for Women, and the Oxford Female Institute (chartered in 1849 and opened in 1850). The combined enrollment for these institutions in 1910 was less than one thousand students. In 1910, Benton Auditorium (now Hall Auditorium) opened and became the venue for these cultural events.

It is quite interesting to note that over the years an extraordinary roster of internationally-known orchestras were featured in the University 'Art Series,' as the lyceum course came to be known. Of special note were the appearance of orchestras from Russia, Dresden and London, as well as from New York and other major American cities.

Miami University records indicate that a rudimentary Department of Music existed at least by 1902. A music faculty member heading the Department from 1902-1903 was A. J. Gantvoort, followed by Dr. Shilo Shaffer Myers from 1903-1907. In terms of research, *The Miami Recensio* and *The Miami Student* newspaper are invaluable sources of information. In the May, 1906 issue of *The Miami Recensio* Dr. Myers makes this comment about the study of music at the university:

> It is recognized that as literature represents the best poetic and dramatic thought of the past and present, so music represents the highest genius and the best social, moral and religious thought in the history of the development of the human race and is, therefore, an inheritance of value equal to any art or science in our educational system.

Following this statement, as the basis for valuing music in the liberal arts, he goes on to suggest that the mission of the Department is to emphasize music education as opposed to a conservatory environment:

> It is not so much the aim of the department to develop the finished artist, as it is to give the student that which is of the most educational value in music and which goes farthest toward developing the best powers which lie within the individual.

Modern society would do well to heed these words of Dr. Myers and ponder his meaning of "the best social, moral and religious thought." One must notice that he does not use words such as 'entertainment' or 'show' to justify music at the university. These are words that often are heard today associated with great music, but this attitude obscures the meaning behind the classical arts.

Some critics today see danger in a prevalent ignorance of the past, and fear that there is not enough attention given to the best social, moral and religious thought. Each time a new freshman class enters the doors of a university, the faculty must be prepared to start all over to shape new minds that know little or nothing about the best social, moral and religious thought. For centuries, the institutions of Western civilization have been working to hang on to meaning and value in human experience, and that effort is probably more important today than ever, in view of society's need for spiritual nourishment. In exploring the meaning and value of music, it is well to remember that a society is strengthened by its musicians and artists, who focus upon the constructive elements of reflection and integrity. Those who sing and play instruments promote a positive impetus in society.

One might also ponder the fact that Dr. Myers, in his *Miami Recensio* article above, speaks of literature as being "the best poetic and dramatic thought of the past and present." We assume that he is speaking of classical literature that endures through generations, rather than literature that is here today and gone tomorrow. In this context, it is wise for today's educators to stay abreast of the best that authors and composers have to offer. This is a task requiring vigilance. It also requires educators to prepare themselves with a firm philosophy concerning such distinctions as the difference between art forms that focus upon entertainment versus those that stimulate thinking and inspiration.

In 1907, Dr. Raymond Burke began a career at Miami as a geology professor. During his student days at Oberlin College he had been a member of the Oberlin Glee Club, and he wanted to establish such a group at Miami. Miami's President at the time, Dr. Guy Potter Benton, was in favor of the idea and invited Burke to take charge of forming a the Miami Glee Club.

The first Glee Club had only eight members, but Burke searched for more singers among the members of Miami's fraternities, finally achieving a Club membership of twenty-one. In 1908, the Club presented their first concert, which included a song developed by Burke that was so successful that it became the Miami Fight Song that we know today. Four years later, The Club premiered another song by Burke that has become Miami's Alma Mater. The 1908 *Recensio* included a photograph of the Glee Club comprised of twenty-four men.

Through the decades, the men's Glee Club has been one of the most spirited music ensembles on campus, a place where steadfast and loyal friendships are developed that last for a lifetime. This uniquely spirited ensemble continues its long tradition into the present day. It provides a spiritual place of strength that brings to campus life the immeasurable value of music in the lives of students. Current information about the Glee Club is available on their website at mugleeclub.org.

Miami University Glee Club, ca. 1908. Image provided by Miami University Libraries, Oxford, OH.

In 1908, Richard Burke formed the Miami Choraliers, originally called the Madrigal Club. It was a chorus of women's voices with membership based on audition. An annual concert was performed each February.

In 1910, the membership was limited to twenty-five women. In 1930, Dean Kratt became Director of the group, which then composed thirty voices focusing on a repertoire of *a cappella* music in three parts. In 1933, Dora Lyon became Director for the next twenty-one years. Under her excellent leadership, the membership and reputation increased as they toured Ohio and were heard in broadcasts over Cincinnati radio stations. In 1947, the Madrigal Club was rated the highest in its field by the National Schools of Music and Conservatories. In 1950, the name of the club was changed to the Women's Choral Society. Everett Nelson assumed the directorship in 1956 and maintained this post until John Wabrick took over in 1964. The name was changed to the Miami University Choraliers in 1965. The popularity of the group up to the present day has resulted in its continuity as one of the oldest musical organizations at Miami University. Today, it has a membership of more than seventy-five women. Their website is found at miamioh.edu/choraliers.

For university faculty members, the learning academy is much more than the average business workplace where deals are made and data is recorded. The faculty and their students form a unique bond that is sealed by a common purpose of exploring the deeper aspects of human life. An example of this

Miami Choraliers, 1909. Image provided by Miami University Libraries, Oxford, OH.

can be seen in how faculty members are often willing to volunteer beyond the call of duty by taking personal interest in students and exposing them to a world of activity beyond the campus. Miami University students were fortunate to have professors who wanted them to learn from cultural events off campus. An article in *The Miami Student* issue of January, 1912, carries this headline: "Many Students to Hear Opera: Rare Treat in Store." The report goes on to say:

> Prof. Burke's class in Musical Appreciation will take a trip to Cincinnati, February 7. The party, sixteen in number, will leave Oxford at 6:41. The class will first visit the Zimmerman Music Engraving plant, where they will see the process of printing music from the original manuscript to the finished product . . . The matinee will be "The Secret of Suzanne" in Italian, and "Hansel and Gretel" in English . . . In the evening Wagner's "Tristan and Isolde" will be presented . . . As the performance will last until after midnight, it will be impossible to catch the train leaving at 11:25, but the sale of tickets from Hamilton and Oxford has been sufficient to warrant the railroad running a special train which will leave Cincinnati about 1:00 A.M.

The article also reports that on this same trip the students were taken to the Baldwin piano factory and the Aeolian Company where they saw fine pianos for sale as well as a large Orchestrelle, "an on organ played mechanically, like a pianola."

The Miami Student newspaper printed an article in its edition of October 2, 1913, announcing the following:

> The Miami band had its first appearance at the game last Saturday. After many hours spent last week in borrowing instruments, searching for musicians, and hounding the post office in the hopes that the new music would arrive, the organization was finally completed . . . It is the hope of President Hughes that the band be made a permanent thing. In order to do this an experienced musician may be employed to conduct and train the band.

Also on record is evidence that traveling musical groups were being brought to campus to add to the cultural environment of the community. An article in the October 15th edition of *The Miami Student* entitled "Lyceum Course Will Be Best in Years," specifies the performers selected for the year and says that "The first number on the program is the far-famed Russian Symphony Orchestra, which will give its concert here on November 9th."

Athletics naturally played an important part at the University. The marching band evolved to satisfy the need for a musically spirited group at football games. It was under the presidency of Dr. Upham that the Miami song took shape.

In the early nineties, a party of which Dr. Upham was one, was on a train going to Cincinnati when, to while away the time, someone suggested that they compose a Miami song. The suggestion was immediately adopted, and by the time the train had reached the city, a poem had been evolved to be sung to the music of "Clementine," which happened to be very popular at Western College at this time.

The Clementine tune was later dropped and the present one adopted.

Chapter Three

Leadership and Music Organizations

1920s

Musicians are rarely wealthy individuals, since their work is more often rewarded by personal satisfaction rather than by money. Horace, in the ode to his lyre, said it plainly: *laborum dulce lenimen* (sweet solace of my labors). Historically, during former centuries musicians tended to count upon the good graces of their patrons to keep them in business. They were originally considered to be servants in the great houses of the European aristocracy. Franz Joseph Haydn was the servant of the Esterhazy family that employed him for thirty years. In modern times, musicians still tend to rely upon more experienced business-minded people to employ their services. Art, in general, requires patrons to recognize the value of the art and to invest in it financially.

With the crumbling of Europe's aristocracy in the two World Wars of the twentieth century, the old system of arts patronage disappeared. America represented the New World in which a new democratic society saw its own need to protect the arts. Thus, schools of art and music appeared in order to pass on the cultural heritage. These institutions relied upon the education, wisdom and good sense of their administrators to attend to the needs of the arts, since the funding was available for the arts through the institutional budgets.

An institution of higher learning is only as good as the leaders who shape its course. Miami University was blessed during its early years by having leaders with vision and devotion to excellence. Quality in higher education depends upon such leadership. If the achievement of excellence in society is the aim of our time on earth, then certainly those leaders who exemplify dedication toward that goal must be honored. In the early years of the University, it was leaders like Presidents Benton, Hughes and Upham who set the tone of excellence creating the environment for a truly liberal arts institution to grow.

In the 1920s the music faculty consisted of approximately eleven members whose individual years of service spanned five years or less: Bernice Towner, Susan Browne, Ruth Johnson, Roy Williams, V. D. MacGillis, M. L. Nobles, William Ross, Everett Foster, B. J. Keller, Helen Page, and Marin Johansen. In addition, during those same five years before 1929, three members had served longer terms: Joseph Clokey, Aubrey Martin and Edith Keller. The faculty was small but very committed to the ideal of bringing music into the lives of students. The loyalty to this ideal and to the institution that made it possible created a sense of family and added to the growing concept of the 'Miami Family.'

President Upham and the Board of Trustees began planning for a new School of Fine Arts by 1927, as indicated in the Annual Report of the University for the year 1927–28:

> At the meeting on March 9, 1928, the Board of trustees approved recommendations of the President providing for a considerable reorganization of the educational divisions of the University, to become effective at the opening of the next college year in September, 1928. Under this plan the University will hereafter consist of three, and ultimately four general divisions: the College of Liberal Arts, the School of Education, the School of Business Administration, and later, as conditions justify, the School of Fine Arts.

Between 1925 and 1930, there exist a plentiful number of printed programs on file demonstrating increasing musical activity at Miami, including both student and faculty chamber music and organ recitals. In addition, there are programs of visiting professional musicians that lay a foundation for the development of the Miami University Artist Series which was to become one of the finest college series in the nation. Two such programs from the late 1920s were performed by The Mendelssohn Quartet (a vocal quartet from New York City), and a recital by tenor Forrest Lamont of the Chicago Civic Opera Company.

CAMPUS OWLS

The following history of the Campus Owls, a student jazz band not associated with the Department of Music, appeared in volume twenty-seven of the *Miami Alumnus* magazine for the year 1973–74, the year of the golden anniversary of the group.

> In the early 1920s, it was fashionable for Miami's fraternities to rush musicians as well as football players. Young men with various degrees of musical

ability would be found in many fraternities trying their talents in the new field of "jazz" . . . Several of the original members were Phi Kappa Taus . . . During this period, several members of Sigma Alpha Epislon formed a small musical group that entertained at the house . . . They would pile their instruments on a truck and serenade the girls' dormitories at Miami and Western on moonlit nights. The original Campus Owls were organized in the fall of 1924.

The band was enlarged during the late 1920s and began to make annual trips to Europe. The first European tour was in 1927, when the group accompanied the Glee Club. The *Miami Alumnus* magazine reports the following.

> In Paris the band secured an engagement at Zelli's, a night spot that comprised a restaurant and floor show... On Bastille night, a gala occasion, Joe Zelli cleared the tables, brought out the best napery and champagne and toasted the band. The Owls continued their European trips every summer from 1928 through 1939 . . . In 1936, the trip was first class to Yokohama and Kobe, Japan, on the S.S. President McKinley.
>
> The last European trip occurred in 1939. The Cunard ship "Coronia," on which the band returned, had tourist and third class filled with Jewish refugees fleeing Germany. When the ship landed in New York on August 22, 1939, Russia and Germany had signed the non-aggression pact and World War II was on its way.

Some of the members seen in this photo are Patty Whitfield (singer), Keith Irish, Frank Duffey, Al Cool, Fred Walker, John Bean, and Bud Hollis.

The Campus Owls with singer Patty Whitfield, 1938-39. Image provided by Miami University Libraries, Oxford, OH.

The Campus Owls group is a good example of how music creates a strong bond among the members that remains alive for decades. In 1997, a video was made (now in the Miami University Archives) about the history of the Campus Owls. Several of the original members of the group appear in the video telling their stories. They speak to how the group was a family that traveled together and came back to Oxford for reunions and how their paid performances with the Owls supplemented the income and helped pay their academic expenses at the University. One member said that the group was one of a kind that probably will never happen again. By the middle to late 1990s, the Phi Mu Alpha Sinfonia music fraternity assumed the role of managing the Oxford reunions at the annual Miami University Alumni Weekend.

MUSIC FRATERNITIES AND HONARARIES

In 1923 the national music fraternity, Phi Mu Alpha Sinfonia, established the Alpha Theta Chapter at Miami University. The chapter soon sponsored annual concerts. At the time of this present writing (2013), the Alpha Theta Chapter is ninety years old, and it has a membership of thirty-two men. It is expected that the 2014 membership of the chapter will be approximately forty members.

The fraternity is open to men who, through a love for music, can assist in the fulfillment of its object and ideals either by adopting music as a profession or by working to advance the cause of music in America. Members are not required to be music majors. Phi Mu Alpha has initiated more than 150,000 members, known as *Sinfonians*, and the fraternity currently has over 7,000 active collegiate members in 248 collegiate chapters throughout the United States.

This fraternity pledges to assist the Department of Music at concerts and recitals by helping to operate stage lighting and provide general stage management. Unlike most college fraternities, the members do not live collectively in a communal house. They hold regular meetings each semester and act upon chosen projects.

One major annual project for the Alpha Theta chapter for many years was an event held each spring. It was the Southwest Ohio High School Jazz Band Competition and was started by the persistence of a member of the chapter who organized the first festival in the early 1970s.

The secret initiation ceremony to induct new members into the fraternity is often a very moving experience for the inductees, due to the beautiful music used in the ceremony, the powerful symbolism, and the allegiance to uphold the highest musical standards. Part of the mission of the fraternity is to support American music by performing it and occasionally even commissioning new compositions by American composers.

Other fraternal music student organizations include Delta Omicron, a women's fraternity; Tau Beta Sigma; and Kappa Kappa Psi. Like Phi Mu Alpha Sinfonia, these organizations provide a meaningful social framework that focuses upon music in the lives of the members. Music is the common bond in all cases, and the members find their college years enriched by sharing music with their fraternity brothers and sisters. Also at Miami University is a chapter of Pi Kappa Lambda, a music honorary. Its inductees are chosen by a faculty committee based upon academic and musical performance of high quality.

Chapter Four

A Decade of Growth

1930s

The following announcement appeared in the Cleveland News in 1929:

> Oxford, O., May 6: Theodore Kratt, director of the department of music, Fine Arts to be opened at Miami University here next fall, President A. H. Upham announced today.

Theodore Kratt received his music diploma from Becker Conservatory of Music, Portland, Oregon in 1914. He then studied at the Cincinnati Conservatory of Music and Northwestern University. He received the Master of Music degree from the Chicago Musical College in 1929. He also studied music with Rudolph Ganz in Chicago and with Felix Weingartner, eminent conductor and composer in Vienna.

Following 1929, when the School of Fine Arts was established at the University, the music faculty was considerably enlarged. However, some faculty served in the School of Education, while others were attached to the Music Department in the School of Fine Arts. At this time there was a normal school called the McGuffey Laboratory School for training teachers in the School of Education, while music students interested in the art and practice of music enrolled to study performance, theory and composition in the School of Fine Arts.

Printed programs preserved from the early 1930s show the increasing number of musical performances at the University. Theodore Kratt, Conductor of the Oxford Choral Union, led the group in Mendelssohn's *Elijah* in 1933. In the same year we find that there was a University Concert Band that presented a spring concert under the direction of Theodore Normann. By the early 30s, programs were being presented by local chapters of the women's music fraternity, *Delta Omicron,* and the men's music fraternity, *Phi Mu Alpha Sinfonia.*

SCHOOL OF FINE ARTS

Records indicate that the original Music Department (1902–1929) had only a small number of faculty. The early directors were in their positions for only short periods of time until the arrival of Raymond Burke in 1908 and Joseph Clokey in 1914. Burke and Clokey were together on the faculty from 1914 until 1916, and Clokey stayed until 1926, along with two other men whose names appear on record: Aubrey Martin and M. B. Wood.

At the opening of the new School of Fine Arts, Aubrey Martin, Edith Keller, and Everett Foster remained on the faculty of the Music Department, and three new members arrived who would remain on that faculty for several years: Theodore Kratt (1929–39), Edward Mead (1929–60) and Ottis Patton (1929–36). Joseph Clokey had already left to join the faculty of Pamona College, but he returned in 1941. In 1930, three more faculty were hired: Dora Lyon (1930–1968), Christine Cotner-Conover (1930–1946), and Agnes Crawford (1930–1932). At this point, the Music Department consisted of a strong core faculty of nine members.

From 1931 to 1933, four more new members appeared in the Department of Music in the School of Fine Arts, bringing the total faculty number in that division to fourteen. Of these four new members, Allene Herron-Price served the longest term, 1932–1940.

Christine Cotner-Conover received her undergraduate music degree from MacMurray College, a certificate from the Chicago Musical College, and the Master of Music degree from the University of Michigan. She was a fellow of the Julliard Musical Foundation and studied at the Knocker School of Violin Playing in London, England.

Everett Foster received his Bachelor of Music degree from Baker University and a Master of Arts degree from Columbia University. He was a member of the American Guild of Organists and studied piano and composition in Berlin, Germany, at the Chicago Musical College and the Institute of Musical Art in New York.

Edward Mead came with a Bachelor of Arts degree from Harvard University, a Bachelor of Music degree from Yale and a certificate from Fontainebleau Conservatory in France, where he was a student of Nadia Boulanger. He was a Fellow in the American Guild of Organists. During his final three years at Miami, he served as Composer in Residence from 1958–1960. His music compositions were published by the Carl Fischer Company and the Willis Music Company.

Ottis Patton (1929–36) was a tenor vocalist who came with Bachelor's and Master's degrees from the University of Michigan School of Music at Ann Arbor. He taught voice at Cornell College for two years and served as Head of the Voice Department at the Lansing Conservatory of Music, Lansing, Michigan from 1925–29, before his appointment at Miami as Assistant Professor of Voice.

Joseph Clokey was born in 1890, the son of a minister. He spent his boyhood in Oxford, Ohio, and entered Miami in the class of 1912. After studies at the Cincinnati Conservatory of Music with composer Edgar Stillman Kelly, he was appointed to teach organ, composition and music theory at Miami in 1915, a position that he held until 1926. He then joined the faculty at Pamona College in California, where he remained for the next fourteen years. In 1939, he returned to Miami as Dean of Fine Arts.

Upon his return to Miami, he founded a vocal group called the Minnesingers, a group which was later re-named the A Cappella Singers. At that time he also established the custom at Miami of Sunday evening organ recitals. In 1946, he left Miami to become musician at large at Claremont College in California.

Probably no one will ever know how many songs he composed. Four operettas bear his signature. His choral church music made his name widely known, and more than one hundred such works were published of which twelve are in large form. His investigations into ancient church music gave him the reputation of a scholar. Two symphonies, two orchestral suites, various organ suites, and several concerti were among his works. His trips to Mexico inspired him to write Spanish songs. He even commenced work on an Inca Opera. In the mid-1940s Clokey reflected upon the state of Miami's School of Fine Arts:

> It was in 1908 that I entered Miami as a freshman. There was no such thing as a School of Fine Arts in those days. Miami did not offer a single course in Architecture, Art, or Music. Architecture was a kind of side show in Engineering schools. Art and Music were not supposed to have any educational value. Serious students went to Europe for training, while the dabblers took courses in conservatories and academies.
>
> Nowadays there is scarcely a college anywhere in the country that does not give courses in these subjects and on the same level as the traditional academic branches. In most of them, a student may major in the Fine Arts, and the larger schools have established Schools of Fine Arts with their own dean and faculty. Miami recognized the value of these studies early, and her School of Fine Arts places her in the vanguard of forward-looking universities...

The Annual Report of the University for the year 1929–30 made this statement:

Chapter 4

> The School of Fine Arts, inaugurated with the opening of the present academic year, and operating as a basic division of the University, can look back on the first year of its existence with very gratifying results . . . Considerable headway has been made by the School in an effort to cultivate among all the students on the campus an appreciation of the aesthetic values in life.

The student enrollment in music for 1929–30 was as follows: no seniors; one male junior and one female junior; one male sophomore; five women freshmen; and a total of ten special students—six men and four women.

Dora Lyon, born in 1901 in Huron, South Dakota, came to Miami in 1930, with music degrees from the American Conservatory in Chicago. She was then at the beginning of a singing career, specializing in the performance of German Lieder, and especially the works of Erich Wolf and Hugo Wolff. She had also studied in New York with Estelle Liebling, Charles Baker and Felix Gunther, as well as with Lottie Leonard and Conrad Bos. She appeared on programs of national acclaim, including the Lake Placid Festival and General Motors Sunday Evening Hour produced on NBC radio. The January, 1947, issue of *Musical Advance* magazine featured her photograph on the cover. She retired as Professor of Music Emeritus in 1968, after thirty-eight years of service.

In addition to her talent as a musician, Dora Lyon radiated an infectious spirit, and she loved the students. She became an icon of the Department and an advocate of the students, epitomizing the 'Miami Family' image that was part of the entire University. She taught her students in the voice studio and directed a women's choral group called The Madrigal Singers, which she frequently took on tour. She was known for her work instilling stage presence in her students.

Miss Lyon remembered her impressions of the Miami campus when she arrived in Oxford in 1930. She said, "In the springtime I could go to Bishop Woods [where Upham Hall and Hughes Hall stand today] and walk through patches of violets that grew above my ankles." She loved the trees on the Miami campus and enjoyed their autumn foliage outside her second floor studio in old Benton Hall, now Hall Auditorium.

Miss Lyon's studio was a place where singers and pianists came together to learn the repertoire of art music for voice and piano as well as aria excerpts from the opera repertoire. In the process of training her students, Dora was a mixture of good humor and discipline. She would say to a student, "Now Dearie, you must eat properly. Remember, food is tone!" Once on a very rainy day in an exceptionally wet spring season, she met her student at the studio door, folding her umbrella. The student asked what she thought of the weather. She replied, "It's nice weather for ducks, but not for Lyons." It was in November of 1963 that the author remembers her working with a student in the studio when someone came to the door and knocked, saying that

President Kennedy had been shot in Dallas. She stepped back for a brief moment and said, "No, this cannot be true!'

The following photo, along with a feature article about Dora Lyon, appeared in the *Miami Alumnus* magazine of May, 1968, the year in which Miss Lyon retired. In the article, Miss Lyon gives her philosophy of music.

> The first thing I believe I have learned is the immensity of the field of music. The second point, the great importance of beauty to man. Third, the role music has in the performing arts . . . My hope is that the University will become more and more aware of the real purpose of the performing arts—and, through this awareness, an atmosphere for studying music, creating music, thinking music, and performing music will be possible. Only then will Miami realize its potential . . . I have tried to instill in my students the desire for creative excellence, to leave the plateau of good-enough for the demanding heights of perfection.

The article gave credit to her gift of teaching and to her students who had singing careers in New York, Boston and Germany. An excerpt from the article reads,

> One of America's truly gifted teachers of voice has retired from the faculty of Miami University after a career of immense production and satisfaction. Professional vocalists in many parts of the world claim Dora Lyon as the person who, more than all others, provided the early confidence, dedication to music, and sense of musical values upon which their present professional careers are based.
>
> It is impossible to list all of the established professionals taught by Miss Lyon, but a cross section includes Bes-Arlene '63, now in New York; Alis Manukayan '60, Istanbul; Linda Sanford, '55, Boston; Kaye Krafft '62, Munich; and Mary Ingram '64, New York.

In the same issue of the magazine was a photo and article about Miss Lyon's student, Bes-Arlene Crase.

> Known as Bes-Arlene Crase in her undergraduate days, Bes-Arlene is an enterprising young vocalist whose original home was nearby Hamilton, Ohio . . . Alumni from coast to coast may recognize the young coloratura from her work on the Bell Telephone Hour. Others may have seen her on Broadway in the musical *Skits-Oh-Frantics*, or in the motion picture *Across the River*. . .

In 1936, three more faculty members came to the Music Department: George F. Barron, W. H. Heermann, Isabel Clark and Alfred Lekvold. Heermann stayed for only two years, but Barron, Clark and Lekvold became longstanding faculty members. Three more faculty were hired during the years 1937–1939: N. T. Fisher and Emil Schmachtenberg (both of whom stayed for two years), M. E. Schienetz (one year), and Joseph Clokey. Clokey served as a core faculty member from 1941 until his retirement in 1950.

Chapter 4

Dora Lyon Retires

"The first thing I believe I have learned is the immensity of the field of music. The second point, the great importance of beauty to man. Third, the role music has in the performing arts. This is our challenge. God has given man talent and the ability to communicate beauty. My hope is that the university will become more and more aware of the real purpose of the performing arts—and, through this awareness, an atmosphere for studying music, creating music, thinking music, and performing music will be possible. Only then will Miami realize its potential."

ONE OF AMERICA'S TRULY GIFTED TEACHERS of voice has retired from the faculty of Miami University after a career of immense production and satisfaction. Professional vocalists in many parts of the world claim Dora Lyon as the person who, more than all others, provided the early confidence, dedication to music, and sense of musical values upon which their present professional careers are based.

It is impossible to list all of the established professionals taught by Miss Lyon, but a cross section includes Bes-Arlene '63, now in New York; Alis Manukayan '60, Istanbul; Linda Sanford, '55, Boston; Kaye Krafft '62, Munich; and Mary Ingram '64, New York.

"Teaching is not difficult," observes Miss Lyon. "Nurturing an inxorable demand for perfection poses the challenge in music as in every discipline, every art, every part of life that is worth living. I have tried to instill in my students the desire for creative excellence, to leave the plateau of good-enough for the demanding heights of perfection."

Miami Alumnus magazine, May 1968. Image provided by Miami University libraries, Oxford, OH.

George F. Barron was educated at the University of Oregon and did private study in New York City at the Juilliard School of Music and in Vienna, Austria. As a professional singer, he performed on the Cesare Sodero Operatic Hour on the Mutual Radio Network and at the Church of the Assumption in New York City. He served on the music faculty from 1936 until his retirement in 1973. He was Director of the Miami Men's Glee Club and a teacher of voice from 1936 to 1952. He served as Dean of the School of Fine Arts from 1954 until 1973 and also as Director of the *A Cappella Singers,* a major choral organization that was part of the music curriculum in the Department of Music. In 1968, the *A Cappella Singers* joined the Cincinnati Symphony Orchestra and the world-famous composer-pianist, Dave Brubeck, in a world premiere of Brubeck's *The Light in the Wilderness.* Barron was appointed Director of the University Artists Series in 1961.

Isabel Clark remained on the music faculty from her arrival in 1936 until her retirement in 1960. After early musical training in Portland Oregon, she went to the New England Conservatory in Boston, Massachusetts, in 1914, where she received the Soloist's Diploma in piano in 1915. Her teaching positions before coming to Miami University were at the Blue Mountain College and Hillman College in Mississippi and at the University of Idaho at Moscow, Idaho. She was known as a superb teacher and performer.

SCHOOL OF EDUCATION

In the School of Education beginning in 1929, several music faculty appear on record serving for brief periods. The two longest-serving members were Theodore Normann and Hellen Holl. Normann joined the music education faculty in 1932 and resigned in 1936. As Head of the Department of Music Education, Normann developed a student recruitment letter in the 1930s that was sent to prospective music education students. An excerpt from the letter is quoted below.

> We in the department, feel that there is no line of human endeavor which holds greater possibilities for enjoyable living and genuine service. Our mission is to bring beauty, joy, and an enriched life to others. The field of music education extends from the school room to the community recreational director, from teaching music to little children to the fields of radio, orchestra, band, and choral conducting . . . This fall the music department will have the use of Presser Hall, one of the finest and most up-to-date buildings in the country. The building is new, containing in addition to beautiful and well-equipped studios, 36 rooms with pianos for practice purposes, and a concert hall equipped with a $60,000, four-manual Skinner organ . . . The musical fare of Cincinnati is made available to students through special trips . . .

Hellen Holl came with a Bachelor of Science degree from the University of Idaho, a Bachelor of Music from the American Conservatory of Music, and a Master of Music degree from Northwestern University. Then, from 1936–1938 four new music education faculty arrived who would continue their positions as core music education faculty for a number of years: Alfred Lekvold (1936–1966); Catherine Adams (1937–1946); Helen Page (1937–1953); and Eileen McMillan (1938–1947). Lekvold came with a Bachelor of Arts and a Music Diploma from South Dakota State College, a Bachelor of Arts in Music Education from MacPhail School of Music and a Master of Arts from Columbia University.

Chapter Five

Further Expansion of the Department

1940s

Printed programs from the early 1940s illustrate increasing student performance activity in the Department. The University Symphony Orchestra performed a series of 'Pop Concerts,' and the choral groups such as The Minnesingers and The Madrigal Club presented annual performances. In 1944, the *German Requiem* of Johannes Brahms was performed featuring The Minnesingers and the University Symphony Orchestra.

The 1940s also saw a movement toward bringing international artists to Miami and the building of the Miami University Artists Series. In March, 1948, Dean Gordon Sutherland, in cooperation with The Elizabeth Sprague Coolidge Foundation at the Library of Congress, brought the renowned London String Quartet from England to Miami for a residency of several days performing concerts in Benton Auditorium (now Hall Auditorium). One of the concerts featured two Miami faculty members, Elizabeth Potteiger and Louise Erickson, performing with the London String Quartet.

MUSIC EDUCATION

During the first five years of the 1940s, six music education faculty members were hired in the School of Education, five of whom stayed for very short terms of service. However, in 1945, Alberta Lutz-Ittel was appointed to the faculty and became a core faculty member in music education for the next three decades.

In the second half of the 1940s, up to 1949, four new music faculty members in the School of Education served for short periods. A fifth new person, Harold Mohr, was appointed to the music education faculty in 1949 and remained until his retirement in 1971. His degrees in music education were from Miami University (1929) and Ohio State University (1937).

Then in 1950, Lois Lehmkuhl came to join the music education faculty. She served the longest continuous tenure of any music faculty ever to be employed in music at Miami. She retired in 2001 after fifty years of service. Nearly half a century after her arrival at Miami, she once told the story of her interview for the job, revealing how the world had changed during those fifty years.

> I took the train from Long Island, New York, where I had been teaching and arrived at the Union Terminal train station in Cincinnati where Gordon Sutherland, Miami's Dean of Fine Arts drove from Oxford to chauffer me back to the campus for the interview. I deposited a coin into the door of a private shower cabana at the station where travelers could take a shower after a long train trip.
>
> I dressed for the interview and put on long-sleeve gloves and a hat. The decorum of the day required a woman always to wear gloves on such occasions. I was then driven to Oxford for the interview.

Lois will always be remembered as one of the most colorful members of the music faculty, due to her combination of strictness and conventionality mixed with a love of good humor and, at times, the risqué. She enjoyed telling everyone that she hailed from a tiny town in Iowa called Quasqueton-on-the-Wapsipinicon. Her initial duties at Miami involved teaching at the McGuffey Laboratory School and supervising the practice teachers there. One of her students from those years remembers being afraid of her because of her strict way of maintaining discipline. At the time of her retirement, she had the distinction of having taught at Miami University for fifty years.

Miss Lehmkuhl was a champion of the underdog. She often referred to faculty members as being workers 'down in the trenches,' as she put it. She noticed that, as the University grew in size there tended to be an absence of upper-level administrators at Department of Music events. At the time of her appointment to the Miami faculty, there was still in existence the concept of the 'Miami family.' But by the time of her retirement fifty years later, that concept had all but disappeared, and a new attitude of operating the University on a corporate model had taken its place.

FINE ARTS

The 1940s saw a big expansion of the Department of Music faculty in the School of Fine Arts. In 1946 a new Dean of Fine Arts was appointed. His name was Gordon Sutherland. His Bachelor's and Master's degrees in music were from the American Conservatory. His Master of Arts and Ph.D. degrees were from Harvard University. Before arriving at Miami, he taught at Pamona College in California and Grinnell College in Iowa.

According to the music faculty who knew him, Dean Sutherland was a visionary. He realized the potential of the talented music faculty at Miami University, and he took upon himself the task of utilizing that talent to lead the Department of Music into news areas of expertise during the 1950s. An excellent example of this was his conviction that the University needed a resident string quartet of the high quality found at other major American universities. For centuries, the string quartet has been a primary musical outlet for composers. So, it stood to reason that the literature of string quartet music should be represented in an institution of higher learning.

Some of the new faculty members were retained for a maximum of only five or six years. But, four new members hired during the 1940s contributed significantly to the future of the Department: Louise Glasgow-Erickson (1940–1965); Elizabeth Potteiger (1942–1985); George List (1946–1953); Gordon Sutherland (1946–1953); and Elizabeth Walker (1946–1980).

Louise Glasgow Erickson was born in Portland, Indiana, in 1905 and became a pianist for silent movies in Portland. She received a Gold Medal in Piano from the European School of Music in Fort Wayne, at the St. Louis Institute of Music with Gottfried Galston, and at the *Conservatoire National de Musique et de Declamation* in Paris, France. Her Bachelor of Music in Piano at Miami University made her one of the early graduates of Miami's newly formed (1929) School of Fine Arts. She completed the Master of Music at Syracuse University in 1936. After receiving the Master of Music degree, she developed a series of lectures on music for the Master Institute of United Arts, 1936–1940. When her appointment to the Miami faculty began during the wartime years, she gave music instruction by radio to approximately 1600 WAVES. During her tenure at Miami, she presented many solo recitals. In December of 1950, she appeared with the Cincinnati Symphony Orchestra, with conductor Thor Johnson, in the Second Piano Concerto by Johannes Brahms.

Elizabeth Potteiger received music degrees from MacMurray College (1942) and the Cincinnati Conservatory of Music (1945). In 1946, Dean Gordon Sutherland of the School of Fine Arts created a quartet-in-residence called the Miami University String Quartet, and Elizabeth was appointed cellist of the quartet. The name of the ensemble was changed in 1952 to the Oxford String Quartet. She performed with this group for twenty-four years, playing an average of thirty-five programs per year in the Oxford region alone, plus performances for chamber music societies and for regional and national professional meetings. The Oxford String Quartet became the University's musical representatives on concert series in Ohio, Michigan, Indiana, Kentucky, and Illinois. She was Professor of Cello from 1946 to 1985.

Elizabeth Potteiger was very sensitive to students' needs and would go out of her way to help a student succeed. She always defended students, and she reached out to help disadvantaged students find ways to study music. Among her notable cello students at Miami were Dr. Ronald Crutcher, who later received the Doctor of Musical Arts degree from Yale University, and Professor Gary Holt who became a faculty member of the *Hochschule für Musik* in Cologne, Germany.

George List, flutist, joined the Miami faculty in 1946 and continued on the faculty until 1953, when he resigned to pursue doctoral work at Indiana University. He held a diploma from the Juilliard School of Music plus a Bachelor of Science and a Master of Arts from Columbia University. During his post-graduate work at Indiana University, his major professors included Willi Apel, Bernhard Heiden and George Herzog. He was a composer, conductor, music theorist, and performer. Following his doctoral work, he joined the faculty at Indiana University, where he became an authority on South American music.

Lloyd Outland, violinist and conductor, arrived at Miami in 1946, with a Bachelor of Arts degree from Earlham College (1931), a Diploma from the Juilliard School of Music (1934), and a Master of Arts degree from Columbia University (1935). At Miami he served as violinist with the Oxford String Quartet and Conductor of the Symphony Orchestra.

Elizabeth Walker (later Elizabeth Walker Lane) also joined the faculty in 1946, after receiving the Bachelor of Music degree from the University of Oregon and the Master of Music from the New England Conservatory. Like Elizabeth Potteiger, her duties on the faculty included rehearsals and performances with the very active Oxford String Quartet. She retired in 1980.

In an interview with Elizabeth Walker Lane in April of 2013, she expressed regret that she had come to Miami too late to know Joseph Clokey well. She spoke of his dry wit, and related how he presented to the University Senate his vision of a new Department of Music just prior to his departure to California. When Elizabeth Walker arrived in 1946, she befriended Elizabeth Potteiger, who was a student at the Cincinnati Conservatory of Music and was given a grant to teach theory at Miami under Joseph Clokey. When Clokey was preparing to leave Miami, the two women had lunch with him in Oxford. For Elizabeth Walker, this occasion was both an introduction and a farewell to him.

Elizabeth graduated from the University of Oregon and then went to Boston to the New England Conservatory, where she received her Master's Degree in 1946. While in Boston, she was a music therapist entertaining the GIs at nearby Fort Devens. Her main interest, however, was to find a university job. She met with the President of the Conservatory, who recommended her to Gordon Sutherland. Sutherland had recently received his Ph.D. from Harvard and was in Boston looking for faculty to create a resident string quartet at his new position as Dean of Miami's School of Fine Arts. In Chapter 6 of this book, an interview with Elizabeth relates how the Oxford String Quartet came into being.

So, Elizabeth came to Oxford prepared to begin a career as violin instructor and quartet member. She recalls how the quartet evolved slowly in stages. At first, he second violin was Lloyd Outland, who conducted the university orchestra. But Sutherland didn't like him. He thought that he was not a good conductor, and Outland had the habit of inviting townspeople to play in the orchestra in order to enlarge it. Sutherland really wanted to become the orchestra conductor himself, so he did not allow Outland to get tenure.

Gordon Sutherland was an innovator, Elizabeth recalls. Not only did he want a premiere string quartet in the School of Fine Arts, but he also supervised the beginnings of a fine music library. He insisted upon acquiring the complete works of major composers as well as musicological research volumes to be housed in Miami's main library. By the 1960s the library holdings were fully capable of supporting intensive studies in music bibliography. But it was only in 1969, with the opening of the Center for Performing Arts, that a separate music library and a music librarian were established.

Today, the Amos Music Library serves the entire University community by making available music, books on music, and recordings, and by providing reference services for those who would like to have aid in the use of facilities and holdings. The library contains about 47,000 bound volumes, eighty periodical titles and approximately forty-five more available on-line, as well as about 19,300 recordings

Also noteworthy in late 1940s were two new music faculty members in the School of Fine Arts who remained for only two years, but brought significant talent to the Department of Music. They were Leigh Gerdine and Lincoln B. Spiess. Both were hired in 1948. Gerdine left in 1950 to Chair the Department of Music at Washington University in St. Louis, Missouri, and he coaxed Spiess to join him there as musicologist of the Washington University faculty. Later, Gerdine became President of Webster University in St. Louis.

Joseph Bein, who became the violist of the Oxford String Quartet, came in 1948. A year later, George Seltzer was hired. Both Bein and Seltzer remained as long-time core members of the Music Department. Bein came with undergraduate and Master's degrees from the Eastman School of Music. Later at Eastman, he pursued research in the orchestral music of Claude Debussy, leading to his Ph.D. degree in music theory from there in 1969.

Chapter Six

Oxford String Quartet

The arts are very powerful and yet very fragile. They are susceptible to misunderstanding and are as precarious as civilization itself. In the history of Western music great monuments evolved, just as did the great monuments of Western architecture. Virtually every major composer from the eighteenth century onward produced string quartet works of lasting value. It would seem that it is a responsibility of modern society to preserve these monuments, and yet, as time moves on there seems to be an erosion of educational emphasis upon them.

Gordon Sutherland experienced the power of music during his studies at Harvard University, when the London String Quartet performed all of the Beethoven quartets in three concerts. This inspired him to work toward the establishment of a resident quartet at his position as Dean of the School of Fine Arts at Miami University. The word 'inspired' is key to this discussion. The Introduction to this book mentions the role of discovery, intuition and inspiration at work in a community of music students and faculty. A faculty string quartet represents a major performing group within such a community.

Dean Gordon Sutherland was determined to find excellent string players, and his search resulted in the recruitment of Elizabeth Walker Lane, violinist, and Elizabeth Potteiger, cellist. The full quartet personnel evolved in stages until the arrival of Adon Foster, violinist and Joseph Bein, violist. This group of musicians constituted the quartet personnel for almost three decades.

From the early period of the Quartet, the members shown in the photo below are, from left to right, Elizabeth Walker-Lane, Everett Nelson, Elizabeth Potteiger, and Joseph Bein.

The following pages outline a history of the Oxford String Quartet at Miami University from the archives of the Miami University Department of Music.

Oxford String Quartet, Image provided by Miami University Libraries, Oxford, OH.

On January 17, 1949, the reviewer for the Dayton Daily News wrote, "The appearance of a new string quartet on the Ohio scene just over two years ago is good news to devotees of chamber music. How important the Miami University quartet has become in so short a time was amply demonstrated Sunday afternoon at the Dayton Art Institute. Gordon Sutherland, Dean of Miami's School of Fine Arts, is to be commended for assembling such an accomplished faculty."

It was Sutherland, a newly appointed dean in 1946, who had the remarkable vision to make one of his first and most significant acts the creation of a quartet-in-residence at Miami University. This was long before the concept of a resident university chamber ensemble was widely understood or appreciated, and Dean Sutherland had to work hard to win the support of skeptical colleagues. In fact, in the registry of Chamber Music America, only two American ensembles have so far reached their sixtieth anniversaries, both this year: The Juilliard String Quartet and the Oxford String Quartet.

The ensemble formed at Miami University in 1946 was named the Miami University String Quartet. The founding members of that group were Elizabeth Lane, and Lloyd Outland, violinists; Anita Marcus, violist; and Elizabeth Potteiger, cellist. In 1948, Joseph Bein became the quartet's violist, and in 1953, Adon Foster joined as second violinist. From 1950-53, the second violinist was Everett Nelson, who was also serving as Director of the Department of Music-education. The name of the ensemble was changed to the Oxford String Quartet in 1952. The quartet's stated mission was "to bring fine chamber music to students in the University and to make a continuing contribution to the musical life of the region which the University serves." Very quickly, their contribution proved to be much greater than anyone could have anticipated.

An intensive performance schedule in the region began to identify Miami University as a place for serious music studies, particularly in the area of string education, and helped to attract a greater number of talented students to the school. The Oxford Quartet became the University's music representatives on concert series in Ohio, Michigan, Indiana, Kentucky, and Illinois; and it presented on-campus workshops and educational concerts in public schools all over Ohio. Many concerts included joint performances with various members of the Music Department and other invited guests.

In addition to the standard repertoire, the quartet regularly included new music on their programs, including premiers of works by composers Paul Schwartz, George List, and Paul Whear. In 1959, in observance of Miami University's sesquicentennial celebration, the Artists Series commissioned Edmund Haines to composer his String Quartet No. 4 for the Oxford Quartet, a work it subsequently recorded on the CRI label.

In the 1970's, as members of the quartet began to devote more time to the large class of string students they had helped to attract, performance activities declined. The arrival of new string faculty in the 1980's however, brought renewed interest in re-activating the ensemble. Among the recommendations in a 1984 departmental self-study was one that faculty chamber ensembles should be reinstated, a recommendation the new Department Chair, John Heard, was quick to implement. One of his first official actions, in August of 1985, was to re-establish the faculty quartet, at which time he also created a new faculty woodwind quintet. His actions were endorsed and supported by Dean Hayden May and then-President Paul Pearson.

The new Oxford String Quartet's first program was given on December 10, 1985; the performers were Harold Byers and Kiki Bussell, violinists, Marna Street, violist, and Steven Shumway, cellist. Personnel changes since 1985 have included violinists Hal Grossman, Eric Pritchard, Jeff Multer, Susan Walker, Katherine Anderson, and Emma Rubinstein. Mary Harris has been the violist since 1988, with Harvey Thurmer joining the quartet in 1997 and Pansy Chang in 2001. The quartet has been very active, with concerts regionally and nationally, radio broadcasts and recordings, and educational outreach, including the creation and hosting of the Ohio Governor's Institute for Chamber Music at Miami University for 12 years.

In the last several years the Oxford Quartet's activities have also expanded in the international arena. The members of the quartet have served as principal players in the Echternach Festival Orchestra in Luxemburg each summer. This collaboration has yielded a CD with acclaimed pianist Cyprian Katsaris in the summer of 2003. The quartet has toured Argentina and Venezuela in 1997 and 98, and has garnered praise from critics from Cleveland to Salzburg, Austria. Their most recent international tour took them to Korea and Japan, and they have been invited back to perform in Seoul in March 2007. A CD is currently in production with Japanese pianist Masaru Hayashida, which includes the famed Schumann piano quintet as well as the String Quartet No. 3 by Quincy Porter and a rare piano quintet by Japanese composer Koscak Yamada.

The quartet remains committed to the advancement of contemporary music. Composers that have been commissioned by the quartet, or whose works have been premiered by the OSQ, include Samuel Pellman, Elliot Del Borgo, Harvey Stokes, Chet Mais, and Yoohee Kim. An invitation from the Korean Society of Women Composers will form the basis of another Korea tour in 2007.

The Oxford String Quartet continues to collaborate with faculty colleagues and guest artists from around the world. They have collaborated with composers George Rochberg, Sir Malcolm Arnold, Bright Sheng, and Chen Yi, and performed with pianists James Tocco, Frank Glazer, Viktor Chouchkov, Cyprien Katsaris, and Sandra Rivers, as well as members of the American and Cavani String quartets.

The performance of great music obviously requires highly trained musicians who require sufficient time in their schedules to rehearse and prepare complex music for public performance. The uninitiated in society may wrongly believe that string quartet musicians make concert preparations with little effort. However, one must realize that great art is not produced without stringent discipline, coordination and abundant time for careful preparation. Furthermore, such a group of musicians represents the finest examples of discovery, intuition and inspiration that can be shared by both the performers and audiences of a community.

The four members of a faculty string quartet might be likened to a team of scientists working toward the discovery of new ways to think about a subject. The spark generated from their work together guides them toward the unfolding of their purpose. This spark is then transmitted to an audience in a live performance. Thus, the cycle of giving and receiving is complete. One can argue that this process alone is valuable to society. It is a particular human experience unlike any other.

Elizabeth Lane recalls in the following interview how Sutherland contacted her when she was studying at the New England Conservatory and arranged to meet her for an audition.

> I agreed to have the audition at my apartment. So, while I was waiting for him to arrive I went to the back room of the apartment to practice. I was working furiously on the Sibelius Concerto when he came and stood at my front door listening to me practice. Of course, I did not know that he was listening critically. At the conclusion of the interview, I asked him 'When do you want me to play?' He said 'I've already heard you.'

Elizabeth relates the importance of the resident string quartet at Miami University and the vision of Dean Gordon Sutherland.

While Sutherland was finishing his degree at Harvard, the London Quartet played all of the Beethoven quartets there in three concerts. He was excited by that, and after he accepted the job at Miami he invited them to Miami in residence for a time to perform all of the Beethoven quartets.

At the time there were five university quartets (Miami being one) in the country. Besides the quartet at Miami, the other resident quartets in the nation were at Northwestern University, University of Illinois, Indiana University, and the University of Michigan. Sutherland established exchange concerts for these groups to perform concerts at their various institutions. There would be a quartet performance somewhere almost every month during the academic year.

Elizabeth gives the following account of how the Oxford String Quartet became a powerful recruiting tool for Miami University and the Department of Music and expanded public awareness of the quartet.

> We played in every grade school and high school in Ohio. Sutherland published a brochure about the quartet, which was taken to the schools.
>
> We were invited to play on the Miami radio station, WMUB, which was then located in Williams Hall next to Krieger Hall. There was no studio then, so the woman in charge of the project had wires strung from Williams Hall to Bishop Hall, where the quartet played for their first radio broadcast.
>
> Of course, we all dreamed that the University would eventually build a fine auditorium specifically for use by the Department [a dream that as of 2013 had not yet materialized].
>
> A string quartet may function as a recruitment tool as well as creating a sense of community on the campus. There was a time when the Quartet played 'pillow concerts' at the student dormitories in the evenings. Pillows would be provided for the students to sit on in a semi-circle around the quartet as they played.

Elizabeth recalled that the original quartet was in place for almost thirty years from 1946 until 1975. In 1972, Dr. Everett Nelson was Chair of the Department. Elizabeth remembers being called into his office one day to hear sad news. Nelson told her that one of the most difficult things he ever had to do was to break the news that the University would no longer subsidize the Oxford String Quartet. The very last concert given by the original Quartet members was in 1975, including on the program the Mozart Piano Quartet in G Minor, with Louise Erickson, pianist.

During the 1980s, Miami University and its Department of Music decided to re-activate the Oxford String Quartet. The string faculty involved in the new Quartet were Harold Byers and Kiki Bussell, violinists, Marna Street, violist, and Steven Shumway, cellist. Over the next decade, the personnel of the Quartet changed, with the exception of Steven Shumway who remained the guiding force of the Quartet until his untimely death in 2000. Violist

Mary Harris joined the faculty in 1988 and continued as violist with the Quartet through its final year.

Hal Grossman, violinist in the Quartet from 1986–1993, recalls how important the Quartet was for him:

> My years in the Quartet were musically important and rich for me. We did some terrific playing, collaborated with several important artists and commissioned several wonderful new works for string quartet. I was particularly honored to be invited back to play with the Quartet for the 60th anniversary concert of the Quartet in Oxford. That remains a highlight for me.

With the arrival of violinist Harvey Thurmer in 1997, the Quartet enjoyed a period of critical acclaim extending to the international arena. Notable were a series of compact disc recordings and international tours. In addition to tours of Europe and Asia between 1999 and 2005, they performed with pianists Sandra Rivers, Michael Chertok, Anton Nel, and Lydia Brown playing trios and piano quartets. Also during those years, the Quartet mentored other quartets from the Soviet Union and South America. The members of those quartets have gone on to perform in professional appointments.

The vision and support for a faculty ensemble to represent the Department and University underwent a total about-face during 2005. What was so disturbing was that the tour to Asia had met with tremendous support from a variety of University sources, and no sooner had the Quartet returned from that tour than the Dean single handedly cut the funding for the Quartet, thus bringing to an end a flagship faculty ensemble that had been established in 1946.

TERMINATION OF THE OXFORD STRING QUARTET

The Cincinnati Enquirer newspaper carried the following announcement in January of 2006.

> The Oxford String Quartet, Miami (Ohio) University's quartet-in-residence, may be forced to disband, the Cincinnati Enquirer reports.
>
> Emma Rubinstein, the group's first violinist, left the group last year when she married, and her chair remains vacant. Citing budget constraints and declining enrollment for classical music, university officials chose not to create a tenured position for a faculty violinist to replace her.
>
> The Oxford String Quartet celebrates its 60th anniversary this March. It was founded in 1946 and was one of the first quartet-in-residences in the country. Other schools, such as Indiana University and Northwestern University, followed its model. The group has commissioned and premiered new music and toured Japan and Korea last May.
>
> Eighty-five-year-old violinist Elizabeth Lane, a founding member of the ensemble, told the Enquirer she felt "heartsick" when she heard the news.

One long-time musician and resident of Oxford once remarked that she did not understand why the University could spend millions on new buildings, and yet there was no money to pay the salary for a violinist in order to preserve the Oxford String Quartet. The following timeline documents the events during the final years of the Oxford String Quartet.

- 1998: Jeffrey Multer, violinist, takes a leave of absence while playing in the quartet.
- 1999: Jeffrey Multer resigns, Emma Rubinstein arrives in a one year appointment to take his place.
- 2000. Emma's position is confirmed, death of cellist Steven Shumway.
- 2001: Cellist Pansy Chang replaces Steven Shumway in the Quartet 2001-2005. The Quartet plays a concert in Salzburg (reviewed), and tours Korea and Japan with Japanese pianist, Masaru Hayashida, and Korean pianist Phoenix Park Kim (graduate of Miami). The Quartet teaches in Ulsan, South Korea and performs at Yonsei University, Ulsan, and Nagasaki Japan (May 2005). The tour was organized for two years with premiers of several Korean Women composers works for string quartet, teaching in South Korea: Seoul, Ulsan, performing in Seoul and Ulsan and performing in Nagasaki.
- 2005: Fall: During recording sessions in Cincinnati with Masarua Hayashida of the Schumann Piano quintet, the quartet is informed that it will no longer be funded. Emma had returned to make the recording, having resigned from her position in the spring and moving to Idaho. The morning after a long recording session, quartet members meet with the Dean and Department Chair. The quartet is told that Emma's position will no longer be a violin line. Also in that year the Provost and the Dean reallocate the funds ($10,000) that were the sole contribution of Miami University's support for the Echternach project. Provost Ron Crutcher was honored at the Echternach Festival with a medal commemorating the 10-year collaboration of Miami University with the Echternach Festival.
- 2006: This marks the 60th anniversary year of the Oxford String quartet. The Quartet invites violinist Hall Grossman to return and perform in a gala concert where former members of the quartet were honored, including Liz Lane, Adon Foster, Marna Street, Harold Beyers, and Steve Shumway posthumously: all of whom were at the concert at the Oxford Community Arts Center.
- 2006: The final performance of Miami University faculty and students at the Echternach Festival in Luxemburg.

Chapter Seven

A Half-Century of Achievement

1950s

MUSIC IN FINE ARTS

By mid-century, the Music Department, now in the School of Fine Arts, had been in place for half a century. Now it was to attain an even higher level of achievement and reputation. The new music faculty members who were brought to the Department of Music during the 1940s contributed extensively to the success of music at Miami for the next three decades. A core faculty of very high quality had been assembled with a mission of educating their students in the great classics of Western civilization.

These faculty members developed a loyalty to the mission of music at Miami as well as a collegial loyalty to each other. It was certainly the era of the 'Miami Family' that came to be known by all who worked together at the University, both students and faculty. It seems evident that this community of scholars took seriously their collective high-quality contributions to the art of music, and this environment influenced the student body. This resulted in the building of a strong reputation for the Department throughout the state of Ohio and beyond.

A printed program from 1950 documents a performance of J. S. Bach's *St. Matthew Passion* with the Miami University Symphony Orchestra, chorus and soloists. During that same year, Professor A. D. Lekvold conducted a concert of the Miami University Symphonic Band and arranged for Miami University to host the Southwestern Ohio Music Festival. The following memo was sent from Professor Lekvold to members of the upper University Administration.

Miami University will again act as host to the Southwest Ohio Music Competitions sponsored by the Ohio Music Education Association. Solos and ensembles will be held on Saturday, March 18, with about 1000 students attending and utilizing about 10 stages throughout the day. Band, orchestra, and chorus events will be held on Saturday, April 15. About 2000 students will attend that day . . .

Programs from 1951 document the existence of a strong summer music program in the Department. In that summer there was a performance of Mendelssohn's *Elijah* under the direction of George Barron and a concert by The Summer Session Chorus, also directed by Barron. The year 1954 had a busy concert season, including concerts by the Harvard Glee Club and the Radcliffe Choral Society. That summer, there was a Summer Music Workshop featuring band, orchestra and choral concerts. In addition, the renowned pianist Robert Goldsand was appointed to direct a Piano Workshop for four weeks during the summer. The year 1955 was designated as '25 Years of Fine Arts at Miami,' and included many concerts presented by the Oxford String Quartet and the various student music ensembles.

The first half of the twentieth century witnessed an explosion of musicological studies in the major American universities. This seems to have been partially due to the influx of foreign scholars caused by the two World Wars. Many scholars fled Europe to escape the Nazi invasions, scholars like Willi Apel, Karel Husa and many others.

The years 1950 to 1960 saw the addition of a large number of talented and dedicated musicians in the performing and academic programs of the Music Department: George Seltzer, Eugene Hill, Nicholas Poccia, Charles Smith, George Zimmerman, James Riley, Winford Cummings, Richard H. Chamberlain, Adon Foster, John Hardy, Otto Frohlich and Melton Moore.

George Seltzer, with Bachelor and Master of Music degrees from the Eastman School of Music, received an instructor's appointment at Miami in 1949. He then completed the Doctor of Musical Arts degree at Eastman in 1956. During his years at Miami he was a member of the Dayton Philharmonic Orchestra and the Dayton Opera Orchestra, playing clarinet. He presented solo recitals at the Dayton Art Museum, Wilmington College and Earlham College. During the 1960s he published articles in musical magazines, and in 1975 he published his book entitled *The Professional Symphony Orchestra in the United States.*

Lewis Eugene Hill was born in Tornoto, Ontario, Canada in 1909. He received his undergraduate, graduate and Doctor of Music degrees from the University of Toronto He did additional organ study at the Royal Academy of Music in London, England, and joined the faculty of the Royal Conservatory of Music in Toronto in 1941. He was an organist, theorist and composer. In 1950, Dean Gordon Sutherland invited him to join Miami's faculty. In a recruitment letter sent to Hill from Sutherland in July of 1950, Sutherland gave Dr. Hill a candid assessment of Miami's music program at the time.

> I honestly believe that our musical program is now one of the best in this section of the United States; but our strength has grown more rapidly than our reputation. Many of our students would do credit to any institution in the U.S . . . but we do not yet attract these in such numbers that we can skim off only the thickest of the cream. We are very badly housed, in most respects; and are seriously in need of adequate rehearsal space for our choruses and orchestra . . . In short, depending on his temperament, a man can either be very happy here helping to build a distinguished School in an area where I think it fair to say none previously existed; or he can be unhappy at having to work under physical circumstances which are improving, but sill not by any means ideal.

Nicholas Poccia did musical studies at the Eastman School of Music of the University of Rochester, receiving graduate and undergraduate degrees in 1947 and 1948, and did further study at the University of Cincinnati College-Conservatory of Music. At Miami University, he became director of bands and taught conducting and band and orchestra methods. For many years he served as Chair of Admissions Scholarship Committee. He was a member of the Dayton Philharmonic Orchestra, the Dayton Opera and the Richmond Symphony. He gave the following account of his arrival at Miami University in 1951 and the ensuing forty years.

> Prior to Miami University, I was employed at Del Mar College in Corpus Christi, Texas. Gordon Sutherland was Dean at Miami. Without an interview, I was hired on the basis of recommendations from the Eastman School Placement Bureau and two classmates at Eastman who were current Miami music faculty members, Joseph Bein and George Seltzer.
> When I was employed at Miami, I was the Brass Specialist. I taught all the brass instruments. My studio was located in what was called Building #9, a barracks left over from WWII. My tuba class was located in the basement of Benton Hall (now Hall Auditorium). Heating pipes were overhead, and they leaked on instructor and students.
> Dean Sutherland was my Dean for one year. He had accepted a position at the University of Michigan. Soon after, he called me and said "You should come here and audition for the University Wind Quintet position." I appreciated the thought but was happy at Miami. I was able to play French horn chamber music with the Oxford String Quartet, as well as other chamber groups involving the horn.
> 1959 was the Sesquicentennial year at Miami University, and as part of the celebration the Philadelphia Orchestra with conductor Eugene Ormandy was invited to perform. Professor Henry Montgomery called me and asked if I would go to Cincinnati to meet Mr. Ormandy and the orchestra and escort Mr. and Mrs. Ormandy to Oxford. Since I was the University Brass Choir Director, I was asked to write a brass choir fanfare for the event. President Millett

announced that I could not use my vehicle for the pickup. A University vehicle would have to be used and driven by our campus police officer.

On arrival at Oxford, my wife Phyllis and I had lunch with the Ormandy's at the student center (Shriver Center). Dr. Millett came by and was introduced to the Ormandys. After lunch, I was responsible for escorting Mr. Ormandy to the performance hall (Withrow Court) [a basketball arena]. Entering Withrow Court, Mr. Ormandy snapped his fingers to test the acoustics. He turned to me and said, "This will not do." Fortunately, a maintenance person was close by and agreed with Mr. Ormandy that a hanging on the back wall might help. The Philadelphia Orchestra was superb! Ormandy was granted an Honorary Degree.

A reception for the orchestra and Mr. Ormandy was held at the Shriver Center. Because of weather conditions, at the suggestion of the Ormandys, it was decided that my wife and I remain in Oxford. The Ormandys thanked us for serving as escorts and bid us goodbye.

The Miami Artist Series played an important role in our lives. We were able to attend concerts that featured world-renowned artists in all performance areas. We had the opportunity to meet many of them at receptions.

Charles Smith, pianist, studied privately in Philadelphia from 1935-39, studying piano with Isabel Vengerova and Josef Hoffman, and also with Michael Zadora in New York City. He spent five years in the U.S. Army Air Force in the South Pacific, receiving his military discharge in 1946. He then pursued study at Miami University, receiving the Bachelor of Music (cum laude) in 1949 and the Master of Music in 1951, and did post-graduate study at the Cincinnati Conservatory of Music. In the early 1950s, he appeared as pianist in broadcasts over WPFB and WMUB radio stations. He became a major sponsor of the Miami University Performing Arts Series concerts during 1991-93 sponsoring a performance by the Cincinnati Symphony Orchestra with violinist Midori and a concert featuring the Warsaw Philharmonic with pianist Ruth Laredo.

George H. Zimmerman arrived as a student at Miami University following his military service in the U.S. Army from 1943-46. Before the War he had studied organ privately in New York City. He received his undergraduate and graduate degrees from Miami University and was then appointed as an instructor on the music faculty there in 1951. During the following summers he did advanced graduate work in musicology at Harvard University. His teaching duties at Miami included conducting the Choral Union choir and classroom teaching of standard concert literature. Following his years at Miami, he moved to Dayton, Ohio, where he became Supervisor of Music in the Dayton Public Schools and later was a full-time Lecturer at the University of Dayton.

Winford "Jack" Cummings joined the Miami faculty in 1953 when he was actively recruited from Southern Methodist University. He was a nationally known scholar and researcher, a gifted violinist, an active conductor and composer, a music theorist, and a free-lance editor. He received the Master of Arts degree in Musicology from Harvard University in 1949, where he studied with internationally renowned scholars Archibald Davison and Otto Kinkledey, and composers Walter Piston and Paul Hindemith. In the 1970s he coordinated and conducted Miami's Ensemble for New Music in appearances at Carnegie Hall in New York City and the Kennedy Center in Washington, D.C. He conducted this group in works by composer David Cope for recordings made on the Folkways and CRI labels. He was widely known for his work as producer, announcer, and editor of the radio broadcasts "Music from Miami," airing over the University radio station WMUB, in addition to monthly programs for WNYC New York (1953-70) and WCKY Cincinnati (1956-66). He also found time to produce various programs for the Nigerian Broadcasting Company, the Voice of America, and the American Broadcasting Company.

Richard Chamberlain also arrived at Miami in 1953 following graduate assistantship duties at North Texas State College and a position as Head of the Voice Division at Simpson College in Iowa. He was a Fulbright Scholar in Italy at the University of Perugia and the Conservatorio di Milano. He pursued private studies at the Bennington School of the Arts in the United States and in Berlin and Salzburg in Europe. At Miami he was Conductor of the Women's Glee Club from 1953-55.

Adon Foster, violinist, was appointed to the faculty in 1953, coming with undergraduate and graduate degrees from the Eastman School of Music. He left his first teaching job in Kentucky and joined the Miami faculty to help build strength in the string program of the Department and to perform with the Oxford String Quartet. For many years he was Concertmaster of the Dayton Philharmonic Orchestra, which served as the performing orchestra for the Ballet and the Dayton Opera organizations. The author's interview with Adon Foster in the spring of 2013 brought the following response.

> Miami University was one of the earliest universities in the nation to have a resident string quartet. Joe Bein acted as a manager for the Quartet, making all the concert arrangements. In addition to performing at various schools throughout the State, our school concerts also consisted of our speaking to the students and demonstrating our instruments. The Quartet traveled to schools in Cleveland, Toledo, Athens, Dayton and other cities.
>
> I was grateful that Miami allowed me to be a member of the Dayton Philharmonic Orchestra. One reason that I enjoyed the Philharmonic was that it allowed me to attract students to Miami. In those days, the University did not recruit students as actively as today. Recruitment was not a major focus of the Department of Music.
>
> One of my most memorable violin students was Paul Bartel. He went on to have a very successful string instrument business in Cincinnati, but we often gathered together to play string quartets with colleagues. He always has been very kind to me and continues to treat me like a father.

John F. Hardy, clarinetist and flutist, grew up in Nebraska and took an undergraduate degree in music education at the University of Nebraska. His graduate performance degree was from Indiana University. As a faculty member at Miami, he is remembered as an exacting teacher as well as a reliable colleague. The students in his studio responded to his high expectations of them. His colleagues appreciated his willingness to perform with students in special projects.

Melton Moore, following his undergraduate degree from the Cincinnati Conservatory of Music, became a fellowship student at the Juilliard Graduate School in New York City. His Master of Arts degree in music education was from New York University. He left Juilliard in 1933 and worked as a singer and actor in summer stock companies throughout the United States: in St. Louis, Houston, Miami and many other major cities. He performed in the Ziegfeld Follies of 1936-37 and sang operatic roles in three different American opera companies. He did radio and television broadcast performances in New York City, St. Louis, Atlanta, Los Angeles, and other major American cities, as well as in Canada and Australia. Newspaper reviews of his performances appeared in Dallas, Cleveland, Los Angeles, Atlanta, and Boston, as well as The Herald in Montreal, Canada. He was appointed to the Miami faculty in 1959 and retired in 1976. He was called upon during his Miami tenure to serve as stage director for the opera program, and Otto Frohlich worked with him as opera orchestra director

Otto Frohlich arrived at Miami in 1957 and remained until his retirement in 1973. For twelve years he was Professor of Music, Conductor of the Miami University Symphony Orchestra and Opera Director. He was an outstanding accompanist and orchestrator-arranger. He spent many hours coaching young Miami singers. A native of Czechoslovakia, he received a bachelor's degree from the College of Ostrava in 1926, as well as a degree in composition and conducting from the Austrian State Academy of Music in Vienna in 1930. In Vienna he was a pupil of he world-renowned conductor Clemens Krauss.

During the 1930s, he was building a reputation in Prague and other Czech cities. But, with Hitler and Naziism breathing down their necks, he and his wife Herta left Czechoslovakia in 1938, first going to France and then to the United States.

During his career, he conducted opera in Prague and at the National Radio of France. In 1952 he became conductor of the Slavenska-Franklin Ballet Company and the Agnes de Mille Dance Theatre. In 1953 he was invited to conduct two concerts with the New York Philharmonic Orchestra. Also in New York, he conducted the world premiere of Alex North's ballet version of Tennessee Williams' play "A Street Car Named Desire." He toured the Far East with this ballet orchestra, including Hong Kong and various Japanese cities.

MUSIC EDUCATION

In 1951 and 1952, two new music education faculty members were Everett F. Nelson and Richard Schilling. Everett Nelson was born in 1913, when the Music Department at Miami was still in its infancy. Forty years later he was Chair of that Department. He had his undergraduate degree in Music and English Literature from Hamline University in St. Paul, Minnesota, and a Master of Music degree from the University of Michigan at Ann Arbor. During World War II, he served in the U.S. Navy as assistant commander of a Boat Group in the Pacific. In 1947, he entered Cornell University to study under Dr. Donald Grout and was awarded the PhD in musicology. In 1951, he was appointed Head of the Music Education Department in the School of Education and a member of the Music Department in the School of Fine Arts at Miami University.

When Dr. Nelson was invited to write the foreword for this book, he graciously consented and provided the names of several graduates who studied music at Miami during his many years on the faculty. In the foreword to this book, he tells us that the first of his students to graduate with a music education degree was Irving Hamilton, who later became Music Supervisor in the city schools of Hamilton, Ohio. He also mentions other graduates of Miami whom he fondly remembered. Hermon Torge and Bob Monroe became Band and Choir Directors of the Talawanda High School in Oxford, Ohio; David Meeker went on to become Chair of the Music School at Ohio State University in Columbus; George Beverly pursued a career as organist and Classical Music Director of radio station KVXU in Beaumont, Texas; Brian Joyce, who composed a large number of musical works that today are published by Cimarron Music Publishers and Latham Music Publishers; Samuel Reynolds, who as of 2013 was a faculty member at the Miami Education School in Neuberg/Donau, Germany; and Samuel Bennett, who earned the Bachelor of Science in Education from Miami in 1953 and the Master of Music from the Cleveland Institute of Music in 1959. He taught in the public schools from 1955-1970 and then joined the Miami music faculty in 1970, retiring in 1985. Other graduates mentioned by Dr. Nelson include James Miltenburger, Gary Holt, Bill Sliebl, Ron Lawrence, Harry Pingston, and Lee Suman. Some of these graduates are discussed in Chapter 14.

One year after Everett Nelson arrived, Richard Schilling joined the Miami faculty. He was educated at Capital University and Northwestern University. At Miami, he was a professor of both vocal and instrumental music. In 1953, he was appointed Director of the Men's Glee Club. During the 1960s, he was granted a Summer Research Appointment for composing, arranging, editing and transcribing selected choral music for men's voices. He retired in 1981.

Chapter Eight

Merging of Two Faculties

1960s

The fact that, up until 1960, music at Miami consisted of two separate faculties, one in the School of Education and the other in the School of Fine Arts seems unusual. However, the McGuffey Laboratory School, as part of the School of Education, prepared students for the teaching profession that required a specialty of teaching music in the public schools, whereas students in the School of Fine arts followed a curriculum covering the history, composition and performance of music.

The music programs in the School of Fine Arts and the School of Education merged in 1960. From this point on, there would be one single Department of Music in the School of Fine Arts. This merger resulted in a total number of twenty faculty in the Department of Music. The merger was probably a rather major adjustment for the faculty members from both of the once separate music departments. This would have been the first time for these two departments to co-exist. Faculty meetings would now involve the expectations of two somewhat differing points of view. Nevertheless, music at Miami continued to flourish in a liberal arts context that enhanced the quality of education and conferred upon its graduates the ability to become effective advocates for music in society.

The 1960s saw the addition of several more faculty members in the Department. The new members who were to remain and become emeriti were David Bean, John Wabrick, Frank Kunkle, Jerome Stanley, Anne Baxter, Thomas Clay, and Joan Moynagh.

Frank Kunkle, music education, received the Bachelor of Science in Education degree from Ohio State University in 1938 and did graduate studies in music education in 1945. He received the Master of Music degree from

Miami University in 1966, then becoming a half-time instructor in the Department of Music from 1965-1967. He taught in the Talawanda public schools in Oxford, Ohio, from 1967-1974, and was a teacher at the Saint Mary School in Hamilton, Ohio, from 1974-77. From 1977-1981 he was an Instructor and Assistant Supervisor of Music Student Teachers at Miami.

David Bean was born in Rochester, New York, and grew up in Washington, D.C. He took a degree in economics at Oberlin College and also studied there with pianist Emil Danenberg. After his military service, he did graduate work as a scholarship student at the Juiliard School of Music, studying with pianist Edward Steuermann, and received a master's degree. He made his New York recital debut at Carnegie Recital Hall in 1957, and a year later he appeared on the Young Artists Series of the Metropolitan Museum of Art in New York. He made his first European tour in 1960.

Edward Downes, in The New York Times, wrote of his 1957 debut recital:

> He had a beautiful singing tone for the Schubert in the A minor Sonata, Op. 143. He had the rhythmic punch and the bright tone for Ginastera… He caught the grandeur of Liszt's vision of Dante and its poignance, too, which is often harder for present-day pianists.

Harold C. Schonberg, writing in The New York Times about Bean's recital at New York's Metropolitan Museum wrote, "Mr. Bean is a sincere and dedicated musician….a mind of his own and, as the Ginastera showed, a technique to back it up. In short, Mr. Bean is a pianist of real potential."

Mr. Bean was appointed Artist-in-Residence at Miami University, a rare honor for University professors. For several years prior to his retirement in 1984 he was Director of the University Artists Series, bringing to Oxford a host of legendary artists, including Russian pianist Lazar Berman in his American debut (see Chapter 15).

Jerome Stanley arrived as a Graduate Assistant in 1963. Following military service, he returned to Miami in 1969 to serve on the music faculty until his retirement in 2004. He received a music scholarship from the Edwin B. Garrigues Foundation for undergraduate study at Washington University in St. Louis. During these years he operated a private music studio. He won the St. Louis Symphony Young Artist Award in 1962, making his debut as piano soloist with orchestra in 1963. His university training and private studies included work with concert pianists William Schatzkamer, Robert Wallenborn, Stefan Bardas, Robert Goldsand and David Bean. After receiving the Master of Music degree from Miami University, he joined the faculty as Staff Accompanist and chamber musician. His teaching career included instructing students in studio piano, piano accompanying, music theory, ear training, history of theory, and Parallels in the Arts. He did post-graduate work at the

American Institute of Musical Studies in Austria and received the PhD degree in music from the University of Cincinnati's College-Conservatory of Music in 1983. He was awarded a grant from the Ella Lyman Cabot Trust for studies in music therapy at Florida State University, where he completed all of the course work required for the Music Therapy Degree. He taught twice as a Visiting Scholar, in 1979 and 1997, at the Miami University Dolibois European Center in the Grand Duchy of Luxembourg, and also at that Center as a Core Professor during two years, 1987-89. He is author of a book on the life and works of British music theorist William Holder (The Edwin Mellen Press, 2002) and a book entitled *Parallels in the Arts* (Brown & Benchmark, 1995), which explores relationships between visual arts and music. He is also author of *The Pathway Beyond* and *A Farmer's Boy*, both published by iUniverse, Bloomington, Indiana. His latest book is *The Making of a Music Academy* (2015, The University Press of America).

John C. Wabrick, tenor vocalist and professor of voice, joined the Miami faculty in 1964, after receiving the Bachelor of Fine Arts and Master of Fine Arts from Carnegie Institute of Technology. Wabrick began his career at Miami in 1964 and retired in 1988, serving as director of Miami's Glee Club, Choraliers, Collegiate Chorale and many musicals for the department of theatre. During his tenure at Miami, Wabrick conducted all of Miami's choral ensembles, founded an all-university choral group and led students on eight European tours. He was named the Miami University Alumni Association's 1993 Effective Educator.

Before his service at Miami, he taught in public schools in his native Pittsburgh and Cincinnati and was a musician in the Army. Among highlights of his work at Miami, Wabrick prepared Miami's combined choirs to perform with the Dayton Philharmonic Orchestra and with opera diva Beverly Sills in Cincinnati. He and other Miami faculty performed at local events as The Four Professors.

In describing his philosophy of education in an interview with Miami's news and public information office in 1993, Wabrick said, "I apply the three f's. In music, three f's means very loud. I must be firm in what I believe students should know, fair in dealings with them, and they must have faith in each other. Without the third one, the first two don't work."

Nancy Runge (whose professional name is Anne Baxter) was appointed to the piano faculty in 1965, coming with a Bachelor of Music from Oberlin, a Master of Music from the Cincinnati Conservatory of Music, and additional graduate work at the Juilliard School in New York City, where she was a scholarship student of Olga Samaroff Stokowski. During the 1985 Bach tricentennial she performed Bach's Goldberg Variations at several universities. Her performing career included appearances at the Phillips Gallery in Washington, D.C.; the University of Illinois Chicago campus; Texas Wesleyan;

University of Oklahoma; the Taft Museum in Cincinnati; and performances broadcast over radio stations WMUB and WGUC.

Also joining the faculty in 1965 was Lee Suman in music education. He had undergraduate and graduate degrees from Miami University. He taught in the Department of Music until his resignation in 1976.

Thomas Clay was appointed to the music education faculty in 1967. His university degrees in were the Bachelor Science from Wittenberg University, and the M.A. and Ph.D. from Miami University. During the early 1980s he was a performing member of the Oxford Brass Quintet. He served as Assistant Marching Band Director and taught in the tuba/euphonium studio. He served the Department of Music as supervisor of music education studies for graduate students.

Joan Moynagh received a degree in English literature from Regis College while pursuing voice studies with Mme. Marie Sundelius and opera training with Boris Goldovsky at the New England Conservatory of Music. After studies at the Pius XII Institute in Firenze, Italy, she was an apprentice at the NBC Opera and appeared with the San Francisco, Dallas, Chicago Lyric, Houston and Santa Fe Opera Companies. She joined the Miami faulty in 1968 and retired in 1998.

INTERVIEWS WITH GRADUATES FROM THE 1960S

George Beverley, pianist and organist, attended Miami University from 1966 to 1973, receiving the baccalaureate in 1970, followed by work in Germany at the Hamburg Steinway Company in 1971. He then returned to Miami and received the Master's degree in 1973. Upon graduation, he accepted a position at Lamar University in Texas and remained there for thirty-one years.

Mr. Beverley is an active supporter of the Miami Men's Glee Club and attends the Club's triennial alumni reunions. He is also active in Phi Mu Alpha Sinfonia men's music fraternity. As of 2013 he was Province Governor of the fraternity's Province 40. In the following interview he shared some memories of his Miami years as well as comments about the 2013 Glee Club reunion at Miami.

> I began my student years at Miami in 1966 before the new music building existed. At that time, the Department of Music was located in Benton Hall (now Hall Auditorium) and an adjacent building named Clokey Hall after Dean Joseph Clokey. Members of the performance faculty had their studios in Clokey. When the first phase of construction began on King Library in 1968-69, the noise so close to Clokey Hall was a big distraction to the music students and faculty. The music practice rooms of Clokey Hall, without air conditioning, were up on the second and third floors and were very uncomfortable in hot weather. It was a relief when we finally moved into the new Center for Performing Arts during my senior year.

> I joined the music faculty at Lamar University as a staff accompanist and part-time classical music director of radio station KVLU. Later, I moved from the position of staff accompanist to full-time director of the station. I have also been a church organist in Beaumont for many years.
>
> The Glee Club reunion this year [2013] was very rewarding. We sang the praises of former Glee Club Director, John Wabrick at the reunion. We have just begun a composer's commission series named after him, and the first composer to be recognized in the series is Rod Nimtz, a 1979 graduate. His composition is entitled "Make a Joyful Noise." Rod is Director of Voice of America Learning Center in West Chester, Ohio.
>
> I enjoyed Miami because it was not a conservatory, but a university. There is a big difference in a conservatory education versus a university education in terms of how life is spent afterwards. Having a university experience broadens one's perspective. The social element and collegiality tend to be stronger at a university, and my affiliation with Phi Mu Alpha Sinfonia music fraternity was very important for me.

Roger Miller, oboist, entered Miami University in 1963 and received his baccalaureate in geography in 1967, followed by a Bachelor of Music degree in 1970 and a Master of Music degree in 1972. His interview in 2013 reveals his thoughts about his Miami experience and his career.

> When I was working on the Masters I started teaching class oboe at Miami and also taught at the University of Dayton and Wright State University. I accepted a position as oboist with the Dayton Philharmonic Orchestra in 1970, and then in the late 1970s I started my reed-making business.
>
> In the days when I taught at Miami University we were never expected to recruit students actively. It was recognized that music faculty performances in the tri-state region and beyond, such as programs given by the Oxford String Quartet, provided a sufficient means of recruitment. In addition, Professor Cummings sent recordings of Miami's music recitals and concerts for broadcast on Miami's WMUB radio station and to a radio station in New York. Also, faculty member John Druesedow had a music program on WMUB on Sunday nights.

Chapter Nine

A New Physical Facility

1970s

It has been pointed out that the building of a major facility of any kind at an institution like Miami University requires an almost magical combination of leaders at all levels of the administration to agree on priorities. Added to that is the need to have private donors on board who are able to support, either partially or fully, such major projects.

The building that is currently referred to as Hall Auditorium was built in 1907-1908 and was known as the Administration Building or the Auditorium. It was the venue for musical as well as non-musical events throughout the twentieth century, and it housed the Department of Music offices and studios until the opening of the Center for Performing Arts in 1969. It was officially named Benton Hall in 1926 after Miami's twelfth president, Guy Potter Benton. In 1969, after some debate about razing the building, it was decided that the building should remain. It was then renamed Hall Auditorium for Miami's fifth president, John W. Hall. It was renovated from 1991 to 1993. The grand opening of the new Hall Auditorium featured a major performance by the Echternach Festival Orchestra, an ensemble of combined Miami University and Luxembourg musicians that was, through the 1990s, an outstanding cooperative project for performances at the annual European Echternach Music Festival. This ensemble, and its unfortunate demise, is discussed in Chapter 13.

Plans for a Center for Performing Arts (CPA) at Miami existed among the Deans of Fine Arts and the faculties of the Theatre and Music Departments long before 1969. Elizabeth Walker Lane pointed out (see her interview in Chapter 6), that in the late 1940s "we all dreamed that the University would eventually build a fine auditorium specifically for use by the Department." In the Foreword to this present book, Dr. Everett Nelson says,

> Of course over the years I heard several rumors about shifts in the priorities of what new building would be next. Several times the Music Building was put lower on the list for different reasons. I never knew about this shifting of priorities as a part of my job. Certainly the Dean of Fine Arts kept pushing for a new building. After years of starts and stops, the University planning and building committee selected the Music-Theater building to be built.

Brian Joyce, library assistant in charge of the Amos Music Library listening center during the 1970s and 1980s recalls how the Department of Music was housed during the early part of the twentieth century:

> Before the completion of the Center for Performing Arts in 1969, the Music Department had never had a building to call its own. For forty years it had scrambled for space, sharing McGuffey Hall with Music Ed, using old Benton (now Hall Auditorium) for performance and practice, teaching in Brice and Clokey Halls (both since demolished . . .), even borrowing space in Western College's Presser Hall. Maintaining any sense of departmental unity was difficult under these circumstances.

A large auditorium had been part of the original design for the new Center but was cut from the final building plan. This was a most unfortunate decision, since the Department of Music had to continue using Hall Auditorium, at the opposite end of the campus, for its large ensemble performances. This meant that the University maintenance department had to provide moving crews to transport instruments and other equipment from the CPA to Hall Auditorium for each concert of the Symphony Orchestra, the Concert Band, the Wind Ensemble, and the Opera.

Since the CPA contained a five-hundred-seat auditorium, named the Gates-Abegglen Theatre, the general public naturally assumed that the Department of Music had a fine auditorium in which to present their larger concerts. However, that theatre was reserved solely for the use of the Department of Theatre, which shared the building with the Department of Music. The University Administration was probably unaware that there was inadequate space, from the very beginning, for two departments sharing the same building. Naturally, the initial result was a rather cool relationship between the Department of Music and the Department of Theatre. Over time, the relationship improved with the changes of department chairs and the eventual moving of the Department of Music to a new building, Presser Hall.

The Center for Performing Arts was the main facility for the Department of Music until the renovation of Presser Hall on the Western campus in 2008. Presser Hall, built in 1931, was constructed to house the music program for the Western College for Women, which had a strong tradition of music education. The building was built at a cost of $150,000, half of which came from a grant from the Presser Foundation of Philadelphia. Theodore Presser was a music educator, businessman and philanthropist who created the foundation, which received funds from his estate following his death in 1925.

After Miami University purchased the Western campus in 1973, the building housed a variety of Miami University departments until the 2008 renovation. Following completion of the renovation, the Department of Music moved its main office and a major portion of its operations into Presser Hall. The Amos Music Library, along with a few faculty studios and classrooms, remained in the CPA, and Souers Recital Hall continued to function in the CPA as the main venue for student and faculty solo and chamber music programs.

STUDENT-FACULTY RELATIONS

The spirit of youth among college students inevitably results in a certain amount of good humor in their attitude toward the faculty. This no doubt is a healthy sign that provides for them an emotional outlet that they can share with their student colleagues. From time immemorial students have sought ways in which to characterize their superiors, and ways in which to play pranks on them. Certainly, the music students from the early days of the Music Department would have shared among themselves their thoughts concerning the members of the faculty. Just how far they might have gone to play innocent pranks on their superiors does not appear in conventional research sources. But, since the author experienced the inside daily life of the Department of Music from the 1960s onward, there are stories to be told that paint a picture of good humor among students and faculty (See Appendix E for an interview with Gary Holt).

Perhaps the early 1970s saw more playfulness in the student body than at other times before or since. There may have been a heightened need for humor at the time. Those years followed closely upon the heels of a difficult time in the nation's history due to the Vietnam War. In the spring of 1970, four students at Kent State University were shot and killed as the result of anti-war demonstrations. During that same month in 1970, Miami University had to close its doors for two weeks due to the spreading unrest related to the Kent State shootings. When the University's doors were re-opened, the Miami students were not the same as before.

Another memory from the early 1970s concerns a one-time historical event in the Department that was apparently inspired by the women in Miami's Delta Omicron music fraternity. At this time, the Miami chapter of Delta Omicron occasionally would sponsor what were termed 'upside down recitals,' in which the participants were encouraged to perform musical works of a humorous or unlikely aesthetic nature. Student performers responded to these recitals enthusiastically. At one point, the idea surfaced that the Department should organize a 'Faculty Follies,' in which faculty members would be invited to create skits to be performed in Gates-Abegglen Theatre in front of the student body.

At first, the faculty seemed uncertain about accepting the invitation, but finally they decided to be good sports. On the given day of the performance, faculty members divided themselves into small groups of three or four. The members of each group met to brainstorm a skit for their group. One such group decided that someone would wear a ballet tutu, and holding a rose between the teeth would do a very brief dance across the stage to the music of Ponchielli's Dance of the Hours. The other two members of the group would dance in pursuit of the rose-bearing dancer, and the whole skit would last no more than two minutes, in order to maximize the surprise element and leave the audience dumbfounded, which was indeed the case at the performance.

The decade of the 1970s brought many gifted music students to Miami University. Elizabeth Potteiger, Professor of Cello from 1946 to 1985, accepted an African-American high school cello student, Ronald Crutcher, who finished his degree at Miami and later went on to become the first cellist to receive the Doctor of Musical Arts degree in cello from Yale in 1979.

Another cello student who received his undergraduate degree from Miami working under Professor Potteiger was Marc Cupkovic, who remembers his teacher fondly in an article published in the *Miamian Magazine* in the summer of 2012.

> She really sort of saved my life and taught me how to see things through until they're complete. She wouldn't let me move on to the next page of music until I really finished what needed to be done.

Charles L. Spohn served as Dean of the School of Fine Arts from 1973 to 1983. His musical training in music education, music theory and percussion was at Butler University in Indianapolis and The Ohio State University. He served as Associate Dean at The Ohio University's College of The Arts and as Dean of the College of Fine Arts at Wichita State University. In the 1960s he directed study to evaluate self-presentation methods of learning in the field of music. His many publications included co-authorship of a multi-volume book series entitled *Sounds of Music*, published by Prentice-Hall. As a percussionist, he performed with the Indianapolis Civic Symphony from 1947-1950 and later became a performing member with the Columbus (Ohio) Symphony.

There were many new music faculty members during the 1970s, including new members at the Oxford campus and the two branch campuses. The known biographies of all visiting, non-tenured and part-time faculty, including the two branch campuses, are listed in Appendix B. This Appendix includes faculty not only from the 1970s, but on into the 80s and 90s.

Samuel Bennett, bass-baritone vocalist and choral conductor, was appointed to the music faculty in 1970 and served as Acting Chair of the Department of Music from 1976-1978. He had received the Bachelor of Science in Education degree from Miami University in 1953 and the Master of Music degree from the Cleveland Institute of Music in 1959. During the 1950s and 1960s he taught in the Cleveland Public Schools and served on the Cleveland Board of Education. As a professional singer, he appeared with the Lake Erie Opera Company and was a member of the Robert Shaw Chorale for nine years. For many years he performed in solo recitals and oratorios. He appeared as soloist in such major works as Dave Brubeck's *The Light in the Wilderness*, William Walton's *Belshazzar's Feast*, Anton Bruckner's *Te Deum*, and Handel's *Messiah*. As a choral conductor at Miami University, his Choral Union ensemble was immensely popular among Miami students from all divisions.

Paul Aliapoulios accepted the position of Department Chair in 1972 following a search in which over one hundred candidates for the position were considered. He was recruited from East Carolina University where he had served as Associate Professor and Assistant Dean. He was chosen as an Outstanding Educator of America in 1971. His degrees were from the University of New Hampshire and Boston University (Masters and Doctorate). In addition to his duties as Department Chair at Miami, he was conductor of the A Cappella Singers. In 1976, he left Miami to accept a position as Associate Dean in the Bienen School of Music at Northwestern University.

Dr. Aliapoulios recalls his impressions of Miami's Department of Music upon his arrival:

> The faculty had many, many strengths and included adjunct faculty from the Cincinnati Symphony Orchestra. The music curriculum was of a traditional nature with very strong basic studies classes in Theory and Music History. Performing organizations which included many students from throughout the University were well balanced and fully enrolled. Choral organizations included many non-music majors. Professor Sam Bennett directed a Choral Union of over 250 students. The choral organizations had the opportunity to participate in the Cincinnati May Festival under conductors Robert Shaw and James Levine. The Symphony Orchestra was at full strength and included a great number of non-music majors.
>
> There were a small number of performance majors; however, they availed themselves of the excellent academic classes offered throughout the University thus well prepared for graduate study. A number of the applied studies Perfor-

mance Faculty members also taught classes thus accommodating the needs of the overall curriculum.

Students pursuing a Music Education Degree had an excellent experience in this program which included strong academics, strong music basic studies, excellent applied study, and wonderful examples of performing ensembles. The surrounding communities also provided excellent laboratory and student teaching experience.

I perceived a number of needs for the department and worked to add new perspectives to the program:

1) An opera workshop was needed to expand opportunities for voice students.

2) It was important to add electronic and computer music to the curriculum. So composer David Cope was recruited to the faculty to establish an electronic studio to benefit all students regardless of their major area of music study.

3) An annual Contemporary Music Festival was established with guest composers visiting the campus to lecture and have their music performed. Included were Milton Babbitt, Donald Erb, and Aaron Copland.

4) A Swing Choir was added to the curriculum, and it performed on the Bob Hope Show that took place on Miami's campus.

5) Other additions to the curriculum were new chamber music opportunities: a percussion ensemble and ensembles for string, brass and woodwinds.

Among many rewarding experiences at Miami, I was fortunate to establish wonderful relationships with colleagues throughout the University, within the administration, within the School of Fine Arts, and the Speech and Theatre Department.

As noted in Chapter 1, jazz music was for many decades not considered appropriate material for inclusion in music curricula at American universities. Likewise, *avant guard* and experimental music lagged behind the conventional classics in college curricula. The Department of Music at Miami was typical in that regard until 1973, when composer David Cope joined the faculty.

Composer David Cope arrived at Miami in 1973 and remained on the faculty until accepting a faculty appointment at the University of California in Santa Cruz in 1978. His degrees from Arizona State University and the University of Southern California allowed him the opportunity to study with composers George Perle, Halsey Stevens, Ingolf Dahl and Grant Fletcher. He was a major contributor to the Department through his development of contemporary music at Miami and his gift to inspire his composition students. He involved students and faculty in rare contemporary music performances such as the *Eight Songs for a Mad King* by Peter Maxwell Davies. Along with Winford Cummings, he developed the Miami University *Ensemble for New Music* and arranged tours for the group to New York City, Washington, D.C., and Northwestern University. The group performed at Carnegie Recital Hall and at a U.S. Bicentennial event held at Kennedy Center in Washington.

The ensemble also released a recording of music by David Cope on the Folkways label.

David Cope has fond memories of his years at Miami University and his colleagues there. Especially important to him was Professor Winford Cummings who worked closely with him in elevating new music at Miami. In the following interview, David gives some of his memories about Professor Cummings. (See also his interviews in Appendix E.)

> Jack "Jocko" Cummings was a colleague of mine for four years at Miami University in Oxford, Ohio. He was a brilliant teacher and loved by his students for giving entertaining lectures and not being easy—a rare combination. He also drank heavily, smoked like a chimney, swore like a sailor, and generally said exactly what was on his mind. Jocko taught musicology, but secretly lusted to be a conductor. I, too, learned a lot from this extraordinary man.
>
> When, after not seeing him for two decades, I learned that he'd died, I was shocked. Not because it had happened too soon, but that he'd lasted so long. For of all the people I'd ever known, Jocko was the most self-destructive. Listening to him late at night wail about his divorce, or how the government had gone to pot, or that life was one big toilet, would certainly convince anyone of that. Not that I wasn't saddened by his death. I was. It meant that many students would not now have the opportunity to take his classes. And that he'd no longer have the chance to teach every one around him about what was what.
>
> His death also reminded me of his native honor. And extraordinary musicianship. As example, during 1974 when I arranged a concert at Carnegie Recital Hall in New York City, I asked him to conduct Varèse's *Octandre*, a difficult piece for eight performers. After preparing this work over many rehearsals, he got the idea that its copyright might cover performance rights and wrote the publisher and performance rights organization responsible for permission. They turned him down. Or, more correctly, requested higher fees than we could pay thus making it impossible for him to go through with it. He needn't have written them, nor even taken their advice for not performing it. After all, publishers and agencies rarely detect individual performances of such little played works. But he did contact them, and then told me he wouldn't put my efforts at risk by going through with it.
>
> In return, I asked him if he would take the very same ensemble and do an improvisation on the musical ideas in *Octandre*, not covered by copyright or BMI. He took my suggestion and rehearsed even harder to produce an extraordinary improvised performance that, while substantially different than *Octandre*, used many of the same motivic ideas and gestures of that work. Even the usually caustic New York City press corps was seduced by his mastery of the idiom in their reviews.
>
> When I heard of Jocko's death and impending funeral and memorial service, I thought briefly of attending, no matter that it was over two thousand miles away. I didn't go, however. For it seemed to me that Jocko himself would not have attended had that been possible. Instead, I decided to remember his parting words to me as I headed to California. "Let 'em have it," he'd said, with a grand sparkle in his eye.

In the 2013 interview with Professor Cope, he provided his memories of two other composers, Karel Husa and Donald Erb, with whom he associated during his tenure at Miami University. Those portions of his interview are given in Appendix E.

Robert E. Lee joined the faculty in 1976. He held a Bachelor of Music Education degree was from Northwestern University and a Master of Music degree from Southern Illinois University. He has published numerous articles on the subject of music education and has given frequent workshops and clinics throughout the United States on computer-assisted instruction in music, music in early childhood education, and the integration of music into the elementary school curriculum. A member of the National Humanities Faculty from 1975 to 1986, Mr. Lee formerly taught instrumental and vocal music in West Virginia, at the Colorado Academy, and at the W. H. McGuffey Laboratory School, affiliated with Miami University.

Ron Matson received Bachelor of Arts Degree (1974) and Master of Music Degree (1976) from Miami University and was highly valued as a staff accompanist at Miami from 1976-2006. During his long career at Miami he served many roles as a conductor, accompanist, organist, piano soloist, choral director, coach and teacher. Elsewhere he served as conductor of the Suzanne Farrell Ballet at the Kennedy Center in Washington, D.C., and conducted the National Scottish Opera Orchestra in a performance of George Balanchine's ballet "Don Quixote" at the Edinburgh International Festival. He has conducted widely in the Cincinnati region and recently celebrated his 30th anniversary as organist and music director of the Central United Methodist Church in Richmond, Indiana.

Sandra Seefeld, flutist, joined the faculty in 1977 and retired in 2007. Her undergraduate degree was from the Eastman School of Music, and her graduate degree was from Northwestern University. She had taken master classes with flutists of international renown such as Jean-Pierre Rampal, Marcel Moyse and Julius Baker. Her performing experience included work with the Fort Wayne Philharmonic Orchestra (Indiana), the Lakeside Summer Symphony (Ohio), and ensembles at the College-Conservatory of Music in Cincinnati, Ohio. She had teaching experience at high schools in New York and Illinois and at Taylor University and Indiana University-Fort Wayne in Indiana.

An interview with Sandra Seefeld in 2013 yielded some of her personal insights about her years on the faculty.

> When I first arrived at Miami to begin building the flute studio, the senior flute students wondered how long I would stay on the faculty, because they had experienced a different flute teacher for each year that they had been there. My arrival established many years of continuity for the flute studio.

I did lots of recruiting in my early years of teaching. But later, the reputations of my students did the recruiting for me. Perhaps the best flute student that I had was Jennifer Lapple, who went on to do graduate work at Yale University.

It was wonderful working with Ron Matson, my piano accompanist for thirty years. He is a fine musician, and I learned more about music from him than from my several teachers. We concertized all over the world.

For twenty-one years I was a member of the Miami Wind Quintet, which was established by John Heard, Chair of the Department for many years. I did a great deal of traveling with the group, and that provided a wonderful learning experience.

A highlight of my career was my sabbatical year in Finland, where I studied at the Sibelius Academy in Helsinki, the largest music conservatory in all of Scandinavia.

Lawrence DeWitt, organist with specialization in musicology and conducting, was appointed Professor of Music, a position that he held until his death in 1996. He was Chair of the Department of Music from 1978 to 1985. He came to Miami from a position as Chair of the Music Department at Morningside College in Sioux City, Iowa. Prior to joining the faculty at Morningside College, he had occupied the position of Music Department Chair at Hiram College (Ohio) from 1962-1970. He held undergraduate and graduate degrees from Hope College (Michigan), the University of Michigan, and Indiana University. During his tenure at Miami University, he continued performing organ recitals in the United States, Canada and Europe. In 1987, he performed in Hamburg, Lubeck, Copenhagen, Stockholm and Oslo, as well as in Washington, D.C. and Atlanta, Georgia. In 1988, he gave performances in New York City, Michigan, and at two cathedrals in Toronto, Canada.

Jack Liles, specializing in music education and conducting, was appointed to the faculty in 1978. His credentials included degrees from Western Michigan University and The Ohio State University and a teaching position as Graduate Research Associate in Music Education at The Ohio State University with expertise in courses related to Marching Band. At Miami he served as conductor of the marching band and the symphonic band from 1978-1997. During that time, he also served for two years as conductor of the Wind Ensemble. He was also Departmental Faculty Advisor and a Supervisor of Student Teachers. He gave freely of his time to conduct a number of musical shows in collaboration with the Department of Theatre. A list of musicals that he conducted from 1980 to 2007, including conducting of operas in 2011 and 2012, is found in Appendix D.

Also in 1978, composer C. James Sheppard arrived at Miami, retiring in 2010. He was trained at the University of Omaha and came with exceptional credentials, graduating *cum laude*. During the 1960s, he received a Graduate Fellowship at the University of Massachusetts and was a recipient of the

Presser Music Foundation Scholarship and the Regent's Scholarship. His musical compositions in the 1970s were published by Seesaw Music Corporation, and Joseph Boonin Music Publications, Inc. He received the Philip Greeley Clapp Memorial Award in Composition from the University of Iowa in 1976.

James Olcott was appointed in 1978 and retired in 2013. His high school years were in his home state of California. His undergraduate degrees were from San Francisco State University. He earned his Master of Music degree from the Manhattan School of Music in New York City. His areas of training were in trumpet performance and music education. Prior to arriving at Miami he taught at Fort Hays State University (Kansas) and the University of Wisconsin at Eau Claire. He had served on the Board of Directors of the Kansas Young Audiences and the Kansas Arts Commission Music Evaluation Committee. During his years at Miami he performed with the Cincinnati Ballet Orchestra, the Hamilton Symphony Orchestra and the Middletown Symphony Orchestra. He also taught at the Blue Lake Fine Arts Camp in Twin Lake, Michigan.

William Albin arrived in 1975 as an Instructor of Music in the area of applied percussion and director of the percussion ensembles. Ultimately, he became Professor of Music and Director of Percussion Studies and Directors of the Miami University Concert Percussion Ensemble and the Balinese Gamelan Ensemble. He came with a Master of Music in Percussion performance from Wichita State University and completed the Doctor of Music degree at Indiana University in 1979. Albin studied with George Gaber, J. C. Combs, Cloyd Duff, and William Platt, among others. Throughout his career at Miami, he remained equally active as a performer and educator. He served as Principal Percussionist of the Cincinnati Ballet Orchestra and Principle Emeritus with the Richmond Symphony Orchestra. He also served as an extra percussionist with the Cincinnati Symphony Orchestra and Cincinnati Opera Orchestra. In addition to symphony work, Dr. Albin performed as percussionist for numerous shows that include: Linda Ronstadt, Liberace, Steve Lawrence and Eydie Gorme, Gladys Knight and the Pips, Sammy Davis Jr., Johnny Mathis, Henry Mancini, the Moody Blues, Ray Charles, and Dennis DeYoung. During the 1970s Albin performed with the Ensemble for New Music assisting with performances and guest artists for the then annual New Music Festival. He also conducted the Miami University Jazz Ensemble II and presented a two-week summer jazz clinic in 1976 with assistance of famed jazz educator, Jamie Aebersold.

Dr. Albin was the first member of the Department of Music faculty to be awarded the Crossan Hays Curry Distinguished Educator Award in 1998. Throughout the 1990s and early 2000s Dr. Albin pursued the study of world percussion music and conducted field research in the following countries: Ghana, West Africa in 1995, South India in 1997, and six field trips to Bali between 2002 and 2012.

Chapter Ten

A Dynamic Period

1980s

The decade of the late 1980s and early 90s was a dynamic period for the Department of Music. Hayden May, who had been Chair of the Department of Architecture, became Dean of Fine Arts in 1983. Two years later John Heard, recruited from the University of Rhode Island, became Chair of the Department of Music. Together, they worked to elevate the Department of Music to a new level of public awareness. It was an example of like-minded leaders coming together to create a wave of progress.

Dean May, like Gordon Sutherland in the 1940s, realized the value of the original Oxford String Quartet. John Heard, when he became Chair in 1985, was quick to implement a Departmental recommendation that the Oxford String Quartet be reinstated, and he also requested that a faculty wind quintet be established. His actions were endorsed and supported by Dean May and then-President Paul Pearson.

In addition to supporting the Department of Music through the channels to the upper University administration, Dean May showed his support of the Department of Music by his regular attendance at music performances. It is not often that a dean chooses to take the time for such attendance, especially when he or she is not a musician. His presence was certainly a morale booster for the faculty.

New Faculty during the 1980s included William Bausano, Claire Boge, Pamela Fox, Michèle Gingras, Mary Harris, John Heard, Haden McKay, Brenda Mitchell, Clayton Parr, Andrea Ridilla, Steven Shumway, Gary Speck, and Robert Thomas.

The appointment of William Bausano to the faculty as a choral director came in 1981. He graduated magna cum laude in music education from

Northern Michigan University and received the Master of Music in choral music from the University of Southern California. He completed the Doctor of Musical Arts degree at the University of Southern California in 1981. As a professional singer, he sang with the Los Angeles Master Chorale and the Roger Wagner Chorale. Dr. Bausano is conductor of the Chamber Singers and Choraliers, teaches voice and choral music courses, and serves as coordinator of the choral and vocal faculties.

Dr. Bausano's musical pursuits have taken him throughout the United States and to Europe, South America, and Australia, performing in such cities as Athens, Florence, Helsinki, Moscow, Paris, Porto Alegre, Sydney, and Venice. He is also active as a baritone soloist, performing in oratorios and operas. In recent years Dr. Bausano has conducted world premiers of commissioned choral works by composers Chen Yi, Ola Gjeilo, Adolpus Hailstork, Joan Szymko, and Corrado Margutti, and Howard Helvey. His choral editions and arrangements are published by Colla Voce Music, Lorenz Corporation, Mark Foster Music, Shawnee Press, Treble Clef Music Press, and others. Prior to his appointment at Miami University he taught vocal music in the public schools in Los Angeles, and at Los Angeles Valley College. Dr. Bausano also conducts the Holy Trinity Episcopal Church Choir in Oxford. He is a founding member, past president, and Honorary Life Member of the National Collegiate Choral Organization.

Pamela Fox was appointed to the faculty in 1982. Her doctorate was from the University of Cincinnati with concentrated studies in music history. Dr. Fox was a publishing editor of the international *Carl Philipp Emanuel Bach Edition* (Oxford University Press) and an authority on American music of the late 19th and early 20th centuries. She conducted extensive research in Boston, New York, Hamburg, Berlin, Brussels, London and Krakow. Her numerous publications include essays in *C.P.E. Bach Studies,* articles in American and British periodicals, entries in the *New Grove Dictionary of Women Composers,* pedagogical articles about American music and multiculturalism and reviews in *American Music* and *The Musical Quarterly.* During her tenure at Miami, she delivered dozens of professional papers at national and international conferences and received many research grants from such agencies as the International Research and Exchange Board, National Endowment for the Humanities and the American Council of Learned Societies.

Also in 1982 Robert Thomas, pianist, joined the faculty, having received the Bachelor of Music in piano performance (with High Honors) from West Virginia University and graduate degrees in piano performance from Indiana University. He had taught as an Associate Instructor at Indiana University and as an Assistant Professor at DePauw University. He came with performing experience in Europe and the United States, including solo performances with the American Wind Symphony of Pittsburgh and symphony orchestras in West Virginia and Indiana. He retired from Miami University in 2012.

Steven Shumway, cellist, joined the faculty in 1983, replacing Elizabeth Potteiger. His untimely death in 2000 shocked the University community. In his youth he had performed as a cellist before audiences in North and South America, Europe, and Asia. His baccalaureate degree was from the University of Kansas and graduate degrees from the State University of New York at Stony Brook and Indiana University. He was a cello student of Bernard Greenhouse and Janos Starker. He served as principle cellist for the National Repertory Orchestra and the Charlotte Symphony and Akron Symphony orchestras. He performed at music festivals in Aspen, Tanglewood, and Grand Teton.

During his years of service in the Department he authored the original Capstone Senior Recital course and worked to re-establish the Oxford String Quartet as a Miami faculty ensemble-in-residence. He was instrumental in creating two tenure-track positions for the Oxford String Quartet. Steven was in demand as a performer and was a member of the Atlanta Virtuosi from 1982 to 1990. This ensemble was commissioned by the National Endowment for the Arts and premiered works by three distinguished American composers, Karel Husa, Gunther Schuller, and Elliot Schwartz.

As a cello professor, his syllabi were well known for being both comprehensive and detailed. An excerpt from his syllabus reads as follows:

> Playing a musical instrument involves every essential aspect of the human experience: physical, intellectual, spiritual, and emotional. Mastering the craft of performance and the art of interpretation requires dedication from both teacher and student.

John Heard, bassoonist, was appointed Professor and Chair of the Department of Music in 1985 and retired in 2007, coming to Miami University with an impressive background. He came with an undergraduate degree from the University of Texas at Austin, and a graduate degree from Catholic University of America, Washington, D.C., and additional graduate study at the University of Arizona and North Texas State University with expertise in bassoon performance. His teaching experience included positions at Trinity University, San Antonio Texas; St. Camillus School, Takoma Park, Maryland; Catholic University of America; and California State University, Fresno, California. His position immediately prior to arriving at Miami was Professor of Music and Chair of the Department of Music at the University of Rhode Island.

Professor Heard came to Miami with an unusual background of leadership expertise and successful teaching in his positions at California State, Fresno and at the University of Rhode Island, as well as an impressive list of solo performances and performances with orchestras throughout the United States. His development abilities in matters of academic staffing and curriculum brought to Miami a wealth of expertise. His managerial abilities included oversight of budgets, development of student scholarships, and work in fund raising.

In California he had developed the Western Collegiate Wind Band Festival, a summer program for Winds and Strings, a Youth Piano Conservatory, a weekly Department of Music radio broadcast, a faculty string quartet, an Art Department concert series, and a host of other successful programs. He was also responsible for developing The President's Quintet at California State University, Fresno.

As a bassoonist, during his tenure at Miami University he made a series of recordings on the Kleos, Helicon IMP Carlton Classics, ProNova, Mastersound, and Oxford labels. Among them was a series of highly acclaimed recordings of bassoon concertos with the National Chamber Orchestra of Ukraine—"Camerata Kiev." An eight-year collaboration of the Miami Wind Quintet and the Prague Wind Quintet resulted in three collaborative recordings in Prague of music for pairs of wind instruments, including first recordings of several works. Also during his Miami tenure were his many international Master Classes in bassoon performance. One of the major accomplishments of Mr. Heard as Chair of the Department was the establishment of an agreement with a major European music festival to give Miami music faculty and students the unprecedented opportunity for European performances—a development that opened the door for Miami's image to be transported across the Atlantic by way of the universal language of music. When Mr. Heard was asked to submit his thoughts about his years at Miami, he outlined the various ways in which he extended the performing opportunities of the Department. His comments about organizing student/faculty exchanges between Miami and Luxembourg are found in Chapter 13. His comments about organizing expanded opportunities in opera and chamber music in the Department are in Appendix E.

The Chairmanship of John Heard brought new life to the Department of Music and a wealth of performing opportunities for its students and faculty. Unfortunately, following Mr. Heard's retirement some of these excellent opportunities did not receive administrative support and gradually disappeared. (See his interview about the Luxembourg Echternach Fesitval Orchestra in Chapter 13.)

Michele Gingras, clarinetist, came to Miami in 1986 with a First Prize in Performance from Montreal Conservatory, Canada, and a Master of Music degree from Northwestern University. She came with teaching experience as a Graduate Assistant at Northwestern University, and as an Assistant Instructor at Indiana University. She also came with major experience as a performer, including Principal Solo Clarinet with the Santiago Philharmonic Orchestra, Chile, the New York Strings Orchestra, and with the Quebec Youth Orchestra and the Canadian Youth Orchestra.

Professor Gingras performed for 20 years with the Miami Wind Quintet, and her many performances as soloist in national and international venues brought valuable recognition to Miami's Department of Music. She recorded more than a dozen CDs, authored and published two books, and wrote 200 articles and reviews for international magazines. During her tenure at Miami, she developed a secondary specialty as a klezmer musician (Jewish celebratory music).

Her research, performance and teaching garnered three distinctions at Miami: She was appointed Distinguished Professor in 2011, Distinguished Scholar of the Graduate Faculty in 2005, and Curry Distinguished Educator in 2002.

Gingras is Past-Secretary of the International Clarinet Association and an Artist Clinician for Buffet and Légère (clarinet and reed manufacturers). She has many videocasts online and hosts her website at michelegingras.com.

Claire Boge, music theorist, came to Miami in 1986 with a baccalaureate from the University of Dayton and a Master's and Ph.D. from the University of Michigan. From 1979 to 1986 she was on the faculty of Hartt School of Music at the University of Hartford, Connecticut. Her cognate studies for the doctoral degree were in Cognitive Psychology. At Hartt School of Music she was a graduate assistant coordinator and advisor and served as thesis advisor. In addition, she served there as Associate Theory Chair, Coordinator for academic computer use, and Chair of the Committee on Academic Standing. Her many published articles and lectures gave her a prominent position among American music theorists. She was nominated during her years at the Hartt School as one of the Outstanding Young Women of America.

Dr. Boge is thoroughly committed to assisting the next generation of teachers, revising her courses every year to best suit the needs of each group of students. She was the 1999 recipient of Miami's university-wide E. Phillips Knox Award for Excellence and Innovation in Undergraduate Teaching, and has earned Greater Cincinnati Consortium of Colleges and Universities recognition as a representative of excellence in teaching. She is coauthor of the third edition of the popular programmed theory textbook *Scales, Intervals, Keys, Triads, Rhythm and Meter (with an introduction to partwriting)*, published by W.W. Norton.

Boge has been active as a founder and leader of many professional scholarly organizations. She recently completed her term as The College Music Society's Executive Board Member representing music theory, and has also been on two different Theory Advisory Boards for that organization. A founding member in the Society for Music Theory, she has been editor of the SMT Newsletter, Treasurer and member of its Executive Board, and a member of its Professional Development Committee. She is also a founding member and Past-President (among other offices) of Music Theory Midwest (MTMW).

Boge has served on the Editorial Board of the journal *College Music Symposium* and has been a guest reviewer for the *Journal On Excellence In College Teaching*. She has also been a Miami University Alumni Teaching Scholar and a member of Miami's Senior Faculty Program for Teaching Excellence.

In 1987, Andrea Ridilla, oboist and English Horn & Oboe d'amore, was recruited from the music faculty at the University of Nevada, Las Vegas where she was also Principal Oboe of the Las Vegas Symphony. Her degrees are from the Oberlin Conservatory of Music and The Juilliard School in New York City. Her oboe teachers have included Joseph Robinson, Louis Rosenblatt, Allan Vogel, James Caldwell, Robert Bloom, Hansjörg Schellenberger, and Maurice Bourgue. She was awarded fellowships to Tanglewood, Yale at Norfolk, the Sarasota Music Festival and the Music Academy of the West. She served as Principal Oboe in orchestras in Las Vegas, Rhode Island, New York, Ohio, and Connecticut, at the Echternach Festival International in Luxembourg, and the Classical Music Festival in Eisenstadt, Austria. She has appeared as soloist with orchestras in Europe, Asia, South America and the USA. Her solo CD, "*L'Amore Italiano...the lyrical oboe in opera and film*," with the Sofia Philharmonic in Bulgaria was released in 2009. *Fanfare Magazine* writes of her CD, "Ridilla plays with exceptional control and a beautiful tone." *The American Record Guide* calls Ridilla's playing "...heartfelt and expressive." With Udo Heng of Reeds 'n Stuff in Annaberg, Germany, she is co-designer of the Ridilla-Heng gouging machine, which is patented in the United States. In April 2012, Andrea was a recipient of a U.S. State Department fellowship to serve as artist-in-residence with the Pacific Symphony in Vladivostok, Russia where she performed with the orchestra as Principal Oboe and as soloist and as a teacher. In April 2012, Andrea was guest artist at the Moscow Conservatory of Music and the St. Petersburg Conservatory of Music performing, giving oboe masterclasses, and reedmaking masterclasses. In March 2012, she was the guest oboe professor at the third *Encuentro* of the *Asociación de Doble Caña* of Seville, Spain. In 2010, she appeared as soloist at the *Musica no Museu* Festival in Rio de Janeiro, Brazil as well as concerto soloist with the *Quito Orquesta da Camera* in Ecuador. She has also been concerto soloist with the Guayaquil Symphony Orchestra in Ecuador, the Festival Echternach in Luxembourg, the Moselle Music Festival in Germany, and the Classical Music Festival Orchestra in Austria. She has been a guest performer in several concerts with Camerata Pacifica in Santa Barbara, California. She has performed solo recitals throughout Italy: in Rome, Florence, Turin, and Pisa. She won the top prize for winds at the Munich Preliminaries of the *Torneo Internazionale di Musica* Competition, and was one of six international soloists invited to Rome for the final round in May 1998.

In an interview with the author, Andrea expressed her thoughts about student recruitment and the building of her studio, her philosophy of teaching, experience with the Miami Wind Quintet, travels abroad, and personal research. Her comments on teaching and performing in Europe are found in Chapter 13. (See also her interview in Appendix E.)

> Concerning my philosophy of teaching, I am fascinated by the evolution of a more international school of oboe playing in today's performance culture. Although it is still possible to discern nuances in national styles, many due to the different reed styles, the oboe world is becoming more homogenous than at any time in our history. This parallels the current globalism trend thriving today. Many current solo oboists in American orchestras were born and trained, in part, abroad. To inspire my students, I perform internationally as much as I can. I encourage students to go to summer festivals abroad to open their minds, broaden their perspectives and to make international contacts. There is so much to learn both in the US, and from our international colleagues. Instilling curiosity and a desire to search for truth in art is a central tenet of my teaching philosophy. In the end, all artists follow their own path, but our youth need a solid foundation from which to deviate. That is what we give them at Miami.

Mary Harris, violist, joined the faculty in 1988, coming with a baccalaureate from Indiana University and a Master of Music degree from the University of Wisconsin-Milwaukee, with concentration in viola performance and chamber music expertise. She came with strong performance credentials including concerto performances in Michigan and Wisconsin and recitals in Wisconsin, Indiana and Tennessee. In addition, she had performing experience with orchestra and chamber groups, including principal violist with the New American Chamber Orchestra and the *I Musici de Montreal* in Canada, a group with which she made three recordings on the Chandos record label. She also performed as co-principal in the Indiana University Philharmonic Orchestra at Avery Fisher Hall in New York's Metropolitan Opera Theater.

Appointed to the faculty in 1988, Gary A. Speck, a native Texan, conducts the Wind Ensemble and serves as Director of Bands. He received the Bachelor of Music and Bachelor of Music Education degrees *magna cum laude* from Baylor University in Waco, where he studied conducting with Richard Floyd and Michael Haithcock. After receiving the Master of Music degree in conducting from the University of Michigan, where he was a student of H. Robert Reynolds, Mr. Speck was a high school band conductor in the Houston area for five years. In 1987 he was a Doctoral Conducting Associate at the Cincinnati College-Conservatory of Music, where he was a student of Eugene Corcoron. The following year he was appointed to the faculty of Miami University in Oxford, Ohio, where he now conducts the Wind Ensemble and teaches courses in conducting, music education, and wind repertoire. Under his direction, the Miami University Wind Ensemble has won praise from numerous composers, including five winners of the Pulitzer Prize: John Harbison, Michael Colgrass, Gunther Schuller, Karel Husa, and Leslie Bassett, for performances of their music. Since his appointment, Mr. Speck has led the Wind Ensemble in eight invited performances for the Ohio Music Education Association, most recently in 2014; five invited performances for the College Band Directors National Association, including the national conference in 1999; at the inaugural Atlanta International Band and Orchestra Conference in 1996; and at the MENC/Michigan Instrumental Music conference in 2005. Mr. Speck is frequently in demand as a guest conductor/clinician and adjudicator throughout the Midwest and in his home state.

Also in 1988, Brenda Mitchell accepted a position at Miami, coming with baccalaureate (Magna cum laude) and Master's degree from Arizona State University, later receiving her D.M.A. from Arizona State. She came with high school teaching experience in Arizona (Mesa Public Schools) and private studio teaching of violin and viola, in addition to performing experience with symphony orchestras in Flagstaff, Phoenix, Sun City, Tempe and Mesa. Her conducting experiences included performances with the Arizona All-Star Orchestras, the Arizona Elementary All-State Orchestra in 1986, and the Phoenix Symphonette Orchestra, a youth orchestra sponsored by the Phoenix Symphony Orchestra.

Dr. Mitchell teaches music education courses at the undergraduate and graduate levels, and serves as the area chair of Music Education and as Associate Chair of the Department of Music. From 1978 to 1988 she taught strings, elementary through high school, in the Mesa Public Schools in Arizona. Dr. Mitchell has adjudicated music festivals and given string clinics in Arizona, Ohio, and Virginia. Each summer from 1989 to 2002 she conducted the chamber orchestra for the Ohio Governor's Institute for Gifted and Talented Students, made up of outstanding high school string players. She received the Doctor of Musical Arts degree in 1994 from Arizona State University. An active violist, she continues to perform in the Cincinnati area.

Dr. Mitchell's research centers around string pedagogy for young musicians. Her publications include three books, *New Directions for Strings, a Comprehensive String Method, Books One and Two*, and *Lessons in Performance for Beginning and Developing Strings*, both published by FJH Music Inc. Published articles have appeared in the Journal of Music Teacher Education, American String Teacher, and Triad. In 2005 Dr. Mitchell received the Crossan Hays Curry Distinguished Educator Award from the School of Fine Arts at Miami University.

Clayton Parr, tenor vocalist and choral conductor, was appointed to the faculty in 1989 and remained until his departure to accept an appointment at DePaul University in 1998. He was a double major in music and physics for the baccalaureate degree from Albion College. He then taught in public schools for five years, later receiving his graduate degrees from Michigan State University. In an interview in 2013, Dr. Parr related an interesting story about accepting the position at Miami.

> I arrived in 1989, rather by accident. I was not really looking for a job. I had completed my doctorate residency at Michigan State University and had applied for both a Fulbright Fellowship and the German equivalent of that. I was waiting to see if I would be accepted for either of these grants. I saw the Miami job posting and decided to apply. I was awarded the Fulbright Fellowship too late, after I had already accepted the Miami position.

He spoke of some of the nation's glee clubs and recalled his work with the Miami University Men's Glee Club.

> The two oldest collegiate male organizations in the country are Harvard and the University of Michigan. There are a variety of ways in which men's glee clubs fit into the various academic institutions in the country. In some places, such clubs are not attached to the music department of the institution. There are other campuses that have had Miami's type of spirit, but not many. One example is Yale University. Back in the 70s, there were some ivy-league groups that were forced to become co-ed. But two examples of clubs that continued as male ensembles are Harvard and Cornell.
>
> During my years with the Miami Glee Club we did a regional tour every year, usually in January. We did two European tours, one in 1993 and one in 1997. There is an important student educational aspect in European tours, and I had to build into our schedule time for students to explore the towns and cities on their own. My idea of an appropriate European tour is one performance every other day, at the most.
>
> We had wonderful venues in Europe, such as Notre Dame Cathedral in Paris and the Cathedral of Cologne, Germany. But, more important were the small town appearances where the men were housed in the homes of local families.

Dr. Parr had some insightful observations about Miami's Department of Music—its faculty, students and alumni—upon his arrival. Especially interesting is his comment about the Department's need, during the 80s, to build upon the concept of quality music performance within a liberal arts institution.

> The 1980s were a difficult time for the Department. When I arrived, there were twenty-six full-time faculty members and only eighty-eight music majors, which was certainly a recipe for change. Not only that, but a questionnaire that was distributed to music alumni by the School of Fine Arts showed that music graduates from the 1980s were not totally happy with the experience that they had. It was a decade in which the faculty had to learn how to recruit students and also had to come to grips with the fact that the Department existed in an

institution with a liberal arts approach to education, which meant the unlikelihood of the Department ever attaining the status of a traditional music conservatory.

By the time I left Miami to accept a position at DePaul University, the number of music majors had risen from eighty-eight to two hundred. It was interesting to me that when I arrived at DePaul, they had between three hundred fifty and four hundred majors with fewer faculty than Miami had.

Dr. Parr's interview concluded with a discussion of music within the liberal arts tradition.

> Across the country, there are different models of music that demonstrate different ways of balancing music education and performance. I was trained in the liberal arts, and I believe that right now is a time in this country for extraordinary opportunity in promoting liberal arts. I say this because of the rapid changes in the market place that are making some vocations outdated. Students will need to prepare for other areas. Also, people are increasingly making decisions about where to live based on the quality of life. A community with an active arts calendar will be an attractive place to live.

THE MIAMI WIND QUINTET

When bassoonist John Heard arrived at Miami in 1985 as Chair of the Department of Music, one of his immediate projects was to create a faculty wind quintet. His idea was supported by Dean of Fine Arts Hayden May, and the quintet came into being as an ensemble-in-residence. The quintet members were Michelle Gingras, clarinet; John Heard, bassoon; Sandra Seefeld, flute; Nicholas Poccia, French horn; and Andrea Ridilla, oboe.

The Miami Wind Quintet performed frequently throughout Ohio and the Midwest and was heard on radio broadcasts in the United States, Canada, Asia, and Europe. Their concert tours took them to China, Canada, Luxembourg, Czech Republic , Austria, and Germany. The Quintet was on the touring artist roster of Arts Midwest and the Ohio Arts Council. Several compact disc recordings of the Quintet were released over the years.

In 1999, the Quintet issued a compact disc as the result of a unique eight-year association between the Miami and the Prague Wind Quintets. Both groups received high critical praise for remarkable unity in style, compelling precise performances, and fine musicianship. As a mark of their collective achievements, the combined ensembles presented concerts by invitation at the Embassy of the Czech Republic, Washington, D.C. and the Embassy of the United States of America, Prague. This unusual association between the two quintets was the first such collaboration by American and European chamber ensembles.

Chapter Eleven

The New Century

1990s and 2000s

Pamela Fox joined the Miami faculty in 1982. A brief biography appears in Chapter 10. She served as Dean of Fine Arts at Miami from 1998 to 2003, when she became the ninth President of Mary Baldwin College in Virginia. As Dean of Miami's School of Fine Arts, and as a member of the Board of Trustees of the Cincinnati Institute of Fine Arts, Dr. Fox was committed to enhancing the School's artistic mission within the University and the surrounding community. As part of that mission, she supported Miami's participation in the annual campaign for the Fine Arts Fund of Cincinnati. In an interview for *The Miami University Report* of April 1999, she expressed the following optimistic views about the arts at Miami.

> We have a really incredible opportunity to make ourselves strong in artistic integration and also to be a national model for doing that. This is a critical time for artistic education because we know that in the 21st century people will need to be prepared to deal with diverse groups and to work collaboratively and across disciplines The arts already offer those models . . .

New Faculty added to the Department during the 1990s and 2000s were Ricardo Averbach, Judith Delzell, John Bercaw (part-time), G. Roger Davis, Kay Edwards, Thomas Garcia, Richard Green, Hal Grossman (visiting), Tammy Kernodle, James Lentini, Jaime Morales-Matos, Mari Opatz-Muni, Eric Pritchard (visiting), Benjamin Smolder, Siok Lian Tan, Christopher Tanner, Harvey Thurmer, Gregory Phillips, and Ethan Sperry.

Judith Delzell was appointed Professor and Chair of the Department of Music in 1990 and retired in 2012, coming from a position as Professor and Chair of the School of Music at The Ohio State University. She had an undergraduate degree from the University of Wisconsin, Madison, and graduate degrees from The University of Michigan, Ann Arbor, where she was recipient of a Rackham Doctoral Fellowship. Other honors included a Distinguished Teaching Award and a Fellowship in Academic Leadership. She came with an impressive number of scholarly publications, papers and major conference presentations, activities as clinician and guest lecturer, as well as a number of important research grants. Dr. Delzell served two different terms as Chair of the Department.

Prior to her appointment at Miami University, she served on the Ohio State University faculty for fourteen years, including seven years as Assistant Director of the School of Music. Her first faculty appointment was at The University of Michigan where she was on the music education faculty for three years. Upon receiving her B.M. from the University of Wisconsin-Madison, she taught instrumental music (grades 5-12) in Wisconsin public schools for five years.

While completing her M.M. and Ph.D. degrees at the University of Michigan, she was the recipient of a University of Michigan doctoral fellowship and the Emil Holz scholarship, and she taught in the university lab band program for five years. At Miami, Delzell taught graduate and undergraduate music education courses, and she was involved in research in policies and practices pertaining to instrumental music education programs, teacher education, and women's studies in music. Her articles have appeared in a number of professional publications, including *the Journal of Research in Music Education, The Quarterly Journal of Music Teaching and Learning, Update: Applications of Research in Music Education, Music Educators Journal, New Ways*, and *The Instrumentalist*.

G. Roger Davis holds a DMA (1990) and a MM in Music Composition from The Ohio State University. His musical background includes extensive touring, playing electric bass with rock and jazz bands on concert and club venues with the Doors, The Allman Brothers Band, The Byrds, and other major popular musical acts from the 1960s and 1970s. Davis has composed music for numerous jingles, industrial films and for television. In 1996 he won second prize for the best industrial film score (for the Panasonic Corporation) in the national Arrow Awards. His art music is recorded on the Vienna Modern Masters, and the Helicon labels. Davis's Piano Concerto in F, composed for Michael Chertock and released on Vienna Modern Masters 3058, received rave reviews in *Fanfare Magazine, The American Record Guide* and *Musical Horizons* in 2008.

Davis was the bassist and arranger for the Global Rhythms World Music Ensemble from 2000 through 2005. The group performed in over one hundred concerts in the USA, including appearances in New York and Detroit with Indian pop music artist, A.R Rahman.

In the 1990s, Davis and his colleague Dr. Claire Boge, presented numerous papers at music theory conventions in the USA. All were based on Davis' adaptations and extensions of Schenkerian Theory for the analysis of Jazz.

At Miami, Davis teaches music theory, advanced ear training, composition and arranging, and the history of twentieth century music.

Gregory Phillips, French Horn specialist, received a faculty appointment in 1990, with degrees from the Eastman School of Music and Bowling Green State University. He had served as Principal Horn of the Toledo Symphony Orchestra and the Midland-Odessa Symphony. In sixteen years with the Miami Wind Quintet, he recorded four CDs and performed in Austria, Canada, the Czech Republic, Ecuador, England, Germany, Greece, Luxembourg, and Venezuela. During those same years, he served as principal horn of the Echternach International Music Festival Orchestra. He has performed with the Cincinnati Ballet Orchestra, the Cincinnati Chamber Orchestra, the Ohio Valley Symphony, the Cincinnati Horn Connection, the Frank Simon Band, the New Studio Big Band, and in Broadway productions.

Ethan Sperry, choral director, joined the faculty in 2000 and resigned in 2010 to accept a position at Portland State University. His degrees were from Harvard University (cum laude, 1993), and the University of Southern California where he majored in Choral Music with minors in Instrumental Conducting, Music History, and Poetry. He came to Miami with conducting experience at the University of Southern California, Santa Ana College, The Roxbury Latin School, and other institutions including the Harvard Glee Club. He was manager of the Harvard Glee Club from 1992 to 1993. He also had teaching experience in the Music Theory Department at the University of California and as a voice instructor at other institutions.

Mari Opatz-Muni, Mezzo-Soprano and Associate Professor at Miami University, joined the faculty in 1996, with degrees from the University of Northern Iowa and ten years of private voice teaching. She made her debut as Nancy T'ang with the Houston Opera in the world premiere of John Adams' opera *Nixon in China*, in which she later performed the same role at the Kennedy Center, Netherlands Opera and the Edinburgh Festival in Scotland. The audio recording of this opera production won a Grammy Award for its national PBS television broadcast and was honored with an Emmy Award from the National Academy of Television Arts and Sciences. In addition, she sang extensively throughout the United States and Europe before joining the MU faculty and becoming the Director of Miami Opera, a position she held for 14 years. During her opera tenure, the opera program won two National Opera Association awards. A complete list of operas produced at Miami University during her years as Director of Opera is found in Appendix C.

Chris Tanner was appointed to the faculty as a Visiting Instructor in 1996 after receiving a B.M. in Music Education degree from West Virginia University and a M.M. in Music Performance degree from Miami University. He founded the Miami University Steel Band in 1994, during his first year in residence as a graduate assistant. After earning his D.M.A. in 2000, also from West Virginia University, he applied for and received a tenure-track appointment in 2001.

As of 2013, Tanner was Professor of Music and serves as Associate Chair of the Department. He is the author of *The Steel Band Game Plan: Strategies for Starting, Building and Maintaining Your Pan Program*, a comprehensive resource covering all fundamental topics relating to the development of a steel band program, and the first of its kind to be published through a major firm. In 2011 he released his debut recording of original music for steel band and jazz soloists, titled *First Impression*. He is a frequently commissioned composer/arranger, and his works are published through Pan Ramajay Productions, Engine Room Publishing, and Panyard, Incorporated.

Harvey Thurmer, violinist, joined the faculty in 1997, coming with degrees from the University of Tennessee, the New England Conservatory, and the University of Miami in Florida. His teaching experience included a professorship at the *Grazer Musikhochschule* in Austria, and the Royal Northern College of Music in Manchester, England. He had served as Assistant Concertmaster of the Miami Florida Ballet Orchestra and played one season with the Colorado Symphony under conductor Marin Alsop. He was the 1979 recipient of the Joseph Silverstein Prize at the Tanglewood Music Festival. He was a member of the Franz Schubert Quartet Vienna from 1983-1989.

Following Dr. Thurmer's appointment to the Miami University faculty as violin instructor and member of the Oxford String Quartet, a series of events led to the ultimate demise of the Quartet. He was hired in 1997. Two years later, the first violinist of the Quartet, Jeffrey Multer, resigned his position, and Emma Rubinstein was appointed to take his place. In 2005, Ms. Rubinstein resigned, and the position that she had held was not continued, thus bringing to an end the Oxford String Quartet.

Tammy Kernodle, with training in Music Education, Music History, and Black Studies, came to Miami in 1997. Her degrees from Virginia State University and The Ohio State University prepared her for additional research in Gospel Music and Jazz History, thus bringing to Miami's Department of Music a wide perspective on ethnic musical values. Her background included several awards and honors, including a P.E.O. International Scholar Award. She came with experience in teaching and the giving of workshops and presentations.

In 1997, Jaime Morales-Matos was appointed to the trombone position in the Department, having received degrees from Indiana University and the University of Cincinnati College-Conservatory of Music. His background included solo, orchestral performances, in addition to international chamber music performances with the Gabrieli Brass Quintet. His teaching and conducting experience included work in Spain, Puerto Rico, Venezuela, Ecuador, Dominican Republic and the United States.

Heather MacPhail was appointed Staff Accompanist at Miami University in 1997. She holds a Master of Music degree in accompanying and a Bachelor of Music degree in piano performance from the University of Cincinnati College-Conservatory of Music. She was a faculty member of the College-Conservatory of Music Preparatory Department for over fifteen years. She is the pianist for Miami3, a faculty trio of clarinet, violin and piano. She coaches undergraduate and graduate piano majors in accompanying, and performs in master classes and recitals with students, faculty, and guest artists. Ms. MacPhail has been the piano accompanist for the Cincinnati May Festival Chorus since 1990. In addition, she currently serves as Music Assistant to Robert Porco, Director of the Chorus, often preparing the May Festival Summer Chorus for performances at Riverbend with the Cincinnati Pops. She is a frequent keyboardist with the Cincinnati Symphony Orchestra, performing on all keyboards.

Siok Lian Tan, pianist, was appointed to the faculty in 1998, with a Performers Licentiate from Trinity College of Music in London, England, and a Doctor of Musical Arts degree in piano from the University of Cincinnati College-Conservatory of Music. She is Associate Professor of Piano at Miami University, teaching applied piano and piano pedagogy, and coordinates the class piano program in the Department of Music. A native of Penang, Malaysia, Tan went to Cincinnati in 1988 as a scholarship student of Frank Weinstock at CCM. She has been heard in live broadcasts on Cincinnati Public Radio Station WGUC and has appeared as soloist with the Cincinnati Symphony Orchestra, Oxford Chamber Orchestra, and Miami University Symphony Orchestra. An active pianist, Tan has presented solo and chamber music concerts in major cities such as New York, Chicago, Luxembourg, Cologne, Cape Town, Hong Kong, Kuala Lumpur, Adelaide, and London, including a solo recital at the St. Martin-in-the-Fields concert series. She performs regularly with her violinist husband, Tze Yean Lim. Tan can also be heard on the recording, *James Lentini: Chamber Music*, released by Naxos. As a clinician, Tan has presented lectures at the College Music Society-Great Lakes Conference, Ohio Music Teachers State Conference, the National Group Piano and Piano Pedagogy Forum, the National Conference on Keyboard Pedagogy, and the Music Teachers National Association National Conference. She has also written articles for the *Piano Pedagogy Forum*, the *American Music Teacher*, and *Clavier*.

Emma Rubinstein, violin, was appointed to the string faculty of the Department in 1999 and served as first violin of the Oxford String Quartet until her departure in 2005, when she moved to Idaho. During her tenure with the Oxford String Quartet, a reviewer in Salzburg, Austria, wrote that the ensemble represented "Quartet art at the highest level." In 1989 she was the founder of the Anacapa String Quartet, based in Santa Barbara, California, and served as first violinist with that quartet until 1998. She had many guest teaching engagements in the U.S. and abroad, appeared on numerous radio and television broadcasts, and recorded CDs in a variety of genres. She was appointed concertmaster of the Idaho Falls Symphony in 2009. She has performed nationally and internationally in locations including Berlin, Paris, Madrid, Salzburg, Helsinki, Stockholm, Seoul, Tokyo and Tel Aviv as guest soloist and chamber musician.

Pansy Chang, cellist, joined the faculty in 2001, having degrees from the University of Southern California, Los Angeles, and Yale University School of Music, where she studied with renowned cellist Aldo Parisot. Her training also included study in London with William Pleeth at the Royal College of Music on a Fulbright Grant. She was semi-finalist in the Leonard Rose International Violoncello Competition in 1993. She came to Miami with an impressive background in chamber music performance, solo concerto performance, recordings, and positions as cellist in the Oregon Symphony Orchestra and the New Haven Symphony.

In 2001, Kay Edwards, music education specialist, was appointed to the faculty, having received an undergraduate degree from Ohio University and advanced degrees from Arizona State University, Tempe, Arizona. Her prior teaching positions were at The University of North Carolina and Oberlin College Conservatory of Music. In her areas of specialization, she had published many articles and projects and had given many presentations including topics of Orff-Schulwerk, Kodály, and Native American Music.

Benjamin Smolder, voice specialist and conductor, joined the faculty in 2002, bringing with him a philosophy commensurate with the long-held objectives of the Department. He says, "I believe great teaching occurs through preparation, research, passion for the subject matter, and love for the students." His degrees were from Alderson-Broaddus College and the University of Kentucky, with continuing graduate work at the Cincinnati Conservatory of Music. He came with teaching experience at Northern Kentucky University, the University of Dayton, the Cincinnati Conservatory of Music, and the West Virginia Governor's School for the Arts. His performing background included oratorios, as well as many opera and musical theater roles.

Ricardo Averbach, conductor, joined the faculty in 2002, coming from an orchestra conducting position at The University of Pennsylvania, and replacing Jose-Luis Novo as conductor of the Miami University Symphony Orchestra. His undergraduate training was in Brazil at the *Escola Politécnica da Universidade de São Paulo* and the National Academy of Music in Sofia, Bulgaria. He received a doctorate from the University of Michigan. His honors and awards included the St. Cecilia Award from Pennsylvania Pro Musica, the Maurice Abravanel Fellowship at the Tanglewood Music Festival, a Governor's Citation from the State of Maryland and an honorary citizenship of Bulgaria due to his contributions to culture. In 2014 he became the President of the College Orchestra Directors Association. His background included opera and symphony orchestra conducting in Brazil, Bulgaria and the United States, as well as an impressive discography and experience in teaching master classes and workshops.

José Antonio Bowen was appointed Dean in 2004. At Stanford University he earned four degrees: a Bachelor of Science in Chemistry, a Master of Arts in music composition, a Master of Arts in humanities and a joint Ph.D. in musicology and humanities. He received a Stanford Centennial Award for Undergraduate Teaching in 1990. Stanford honored him as a Distinguished Alumni Scholar in 2010. In over thirty-five years as a jazz performer, he appeared in Europe, Africa, Asia, the Middle East and the Americas with Stan Getz, Dizzy Gillespie, Bobby McFerrin, Dave Brubeck, Liberace, and many others. His compositions, conducting and playing are featured on numerous recordings. He has written over one hundred scholarly articles for various journals. In 2006, he moved to Southern Methodist University in Dallas to become Dean of the Meadows School of the Arts. In 2014, he became President of Goucher College in Baltimore.

Thomas Garcia, Ethnomusicologist and specialist in Latin American Music, joined the faculty in 2005, having degrees from The Juilliard School in New York, the University of Massachusetts-Amherst, and Duke University. He received chamber music prizes in guitar performance in the Artists International Competition and the National Orchestra of New York Concerto Competition. He had held prior teaching positions at Duke University, the University of Massachusetts at Amherst, and the State University of West Georgia. His scholarly activity included many publications and presentations in addition to performances, musical arrangements, transcriptions and compositions.

Richard Green was Chair of the Music Department from 2005-2011. Before coming to Miami, he was a Professor of Musicology at Penn State University, where he also served as Director of the School of Music, 1998-2004. Prior to that time he was Associate Dean of the School of Music at Northwestern University. He completed the Ph.D degree at the University of Illinois, and continued advanced studies in musicology at the *Technische Universität* in Berlin, Germany. The recipient of several research grants, including the *Deutscher Akademisher Austauschdienst*, he has conducted research on German music of the 19th century in various archives in Europe. He has presented lectures in Germany and throughout the United States to many professional and civic organizations. Dr. Green is the author and compiler of three books, including an Anthology of Goethe Songs (A-R Editions, 1995), and has written numerous articles and reviews on music of the 19th century and music bibliography. He has received several awards for excellence in classroom teaching. He is active in the National Association of

Schools of Music as an evaluator and is currently editor of the College Music Symposium.

James Lentini began his tenure as Dean of the School of Fine Arts in 2007. In 2013 he left Miami to accept the position of senior vice president for academic affairs and provost at Oakland University in Rochester, Michigan. During his tenure at Miami, the name of the School was changed to the School of Creative Arts. Prior to that he was the founding Dean of the School of Art, Media and Music at the College of New Jersey from 2003-2007. His leadership during Miami University's 'Year of the Arts' in 2012 is discussed in the Conclusion of this book.

Miami's President David Hodge commented on Lentini's service at Miami, referring to Miami's newly-named School of Creative Arts: "Jim raised the expectations and success of the School of Creative Arts. He was the one who had the vision for the Year of the Arts, a vision that he pursued vigorously and to great effect."

Lentini, a composer and classical guitarist, received degrees in music from Wayne State University, Michigan State University and the University of Southern California. He has recorded numerous original compositions on the American Classics series of the Naxo label. He received the Andrés Segovia International Composition Award in 2002 for his work entitled *Westward Voyage*.

Bruce Murray, Chair of the Miami University Department of Music as of 2013, holds degrees from Carnegie-Mellon University and Yale University, where he earned both his M.M. and Ph.D. He came to Miami University after five years in the position of Dean and Artistic Administrator of the Bravard Music Center in Brevard, North Carolina. From the time he left Yale until he moved to Brevard as full-time administrator in 2003, Murray served on the music faculty of the University of Alabama, teaching piano and allied courses. He also served in a variety of administrative roles at Alabama and was Director of the School of Music from 1998 until his Brevard appointment. He initially joined the faculty at Brevard in 1993 as a member of the artist piano faculty. He performs regularly at Brevard and continues to teach each summer, primarily in piano literature and other courses. He is also familiar to Brevard audiences as program annotator, pre-concert lecturer, and podcast presenter.

Murray also maintains an active performing career as a pianist and has presented hundreds of concerts as recitalist, chamber musician, and soloist with orchestra. Although he plays a broad swath of the standard repertoire, he is known particularly for his performances of Bach, Beethoven, and Liszt, and for his commitment to new music. He has an extensive resumé in repertoire and world performance.

In addition to his performance, Murray has written scholarly pieces for books and journals, liner notes for recordings, and more than a hundred book reviews for *Choice*. His recordings of the solo piano music of American composer Frederic Goossen are available on the Opus One label. Two compact discs of chamber music with violist Doris Lederer are available on the Centaur label.

Chapter Twelve

Opera and Musicals at Miami

Opera is one of the more difficult programs to initiate and sustain within a music school. It requires the expertise of many different people, often including the services of a theatre department in conjunction with the music faculty. Miami's Center for Performing Arts was built as a facility for both the Department of Music and the Department of Theatre. However, at first there was no official collaboration between the two departments. Music faculty who were hired to operate an opera program had to depend upon their own resources for assembling the necessary forces needed to produce opera.

The production of opera seems to have begun within the Department of Music during the 1950s, with the arrival of Otto Frohlich as Orchestra Conductor. Several voice faculty were already in place by then, and so it was a matter of establishing a cooperative atmosphere among the various faculty members. This was not always an easy task, given the demands of opera production upon faculty time and energy beyond the normal studio and classroom teaching duties.

In January of 1962, the following letter expressing disagreement over the stage director's involvement in the opera program was sent to the upper administration.

> I feel that my position in the Miami University Opera Productions needs clarification if you wish me to continue as stage director . . . I believe I need not state my interest in singers performing, the benefits to them, and the growth of the Music Department that results. It is then in the vocal students' interest, and not as a stage struck thespian, that I offer these suggestions which I feel would make my position with the Opera Department tenable.

The letter then cites the need for all faculty having an equal voice in casting, so that all roles in the opera are made known to all vocal studios, and the best voices are selected for the roles. The faculty member writing this letter demanded that credits pertaining to opera production should be shared equally with the stage director and the orchestra conductor. The letter closes with the following words: "I am happy at Miami and do not want my feelings to change because of bitter inequities. If you do not want me to direct under these stipulations I will be satisfied to return to my vocal work."

During the 1960s, only a few operas were produced, one of which was *Martha* by Friedrich von Flotow. There were years in which the term 'opera workshop' was used to define productions of opera scenes that did not require the same material and faculty resources as full opera staging.

From the 1970s through the mid-1990s, several voice specialists were recruited to the faculty with the double duty of maintaining a studio of one-on-one vocal teaching plus taking charge of the opera program. These positions were not well-designed, since there was no budget allotted to opera, so that the individuals filling the position were almost completely alone in finding resources and support from volunteers in order to stage operas. This unfortunate circumstance was understandably the reason why a number of faculty appointed to this position left Miami after only a few years of service.

One such example of a faculty member 'winging it' to produce an opera was Alma Jean Smith. Her excellent credentials as a candidate for the position included performances in major opera roles with New York's Metropolitan Opera from March of 1974 to April of 1980. From 1981 to 1986 she was the leading soprano in the *Staatstheater am Gärtnerplatz*, in Munich, Germany.

In 1993, as Director of the Miami Opera, Alma Jean Smith accomplished the amazing feat of bringing to the stage a memorable production of Smetana's *The Bartered Bride,* on a shoe-string budget and with the help of volunteers from the Department of Theatre in addition to volunteers from the Oxford Community. Included in the production were children from Oxford elementary schools who had to be trained and rehearsed for acting and singing on stage in a children's choir.

In 1996, Mari Opatz-Muni was hired to direct the Miami Opera and to maintain a voice studio. She became the first long-term Director, holding that position for the next fourteen years. A complete listing of the operas produced at Miami during those years is found in Appendix C. In a 2013 interview, she related the following.

> Two years before I accepted directorship of the opera, the Department brought in a conductor-producer to do an opera at Miami and then take it to the Sorg Opera in Middletown. In 1996 they did *The Magic Flute* . Alma Jean Smith was in charge of the Miami Opera at that time. She had to struggle to stage an opera with practically no budget at all. She had to beg faculty and friends to help.

In 1997, they brought in Charlie Cambopiano, an opera producer and conductor for the Sorg and Whitewater Opera Companies. The opera chosen, *Le Nozze di Figaro*, was a 'joint production' with Miami and his companies. Some of the Miami voice graduate students were serving as interns at the Sorg Opera, but the drive back and forth from Oxford to Middletown was a challenging one because of scheduling and gas money. Pamela Fox, who was Chair of the Department of Music at the time, felt strongly that in order to be competitive with other schools, we needed to do an opera. Initially, I was asked to take charge, but I declined because being married to an opera director/producer, I knew what difficulties were involved and I was not ready to take on such responsibility at that time.

Before I was appointed as Director, faculty member Clayton Parr had agreed to take charge of the opera, but he then suddenly accepted a position in Chicago and left Miami. So I got it by default. We first did *Riders to the Sea* and *The Old Maid and the Thief*. It was a 'workshop' production. Pam found $5000 and said let's see what you can do with this money. Alma Jean was doing the opera, but she had no money to work with.

After the first year, Dean Pamela Fox saw that I could do it, so she gave me $20,000. She asked what show I wanted to do. I said that we should stay away from a foreign language. It was clear that *Albert Herring* would be a good first opera. I didn't realize that each score was $85 plus paying the per-performance royalties for Benjamin Britton. You are not allowed to make any cuts.

At first, I rented sets from another state. I had to pay a driver to go and get it. We had to pay $10,000 to get the set here. It was a very large set, and it had to fit Hall Auditorium, which has its limitations. So, I had to hire the original designer as consultant to cut and fit the set. He literally made cut-out pieces of the set in order to fit it to the stage. We kept the same budget for ten years. And then I realized that I could not get more money out of the School.

I got permission to fund-raise. I started with Cincinnati Opera people and some Miami people. Some groups in the Department were upset because I got to fund-raise and they didn't. Once in a while we were successful with business donors but not corporate donors.

To draw voice students to the Department, we need to have opera. Students are very critical now, so they look at schools carefully. The more operatic experience they get, the happier they are. So, opera here was a recruitment tool because of our small department that allows students singing opportunity beyond the choral organizations. The quality has risen dramatically. Most of the students are now strong.

Dr. Fox gave me a load release. When I first came, opera was in the spring. But when opera changed to the fall, then I had to use my summer to oversee the progress. It was so expensive to truck a set here, we had to design the sets here and build them in the summer. I hired designers from CCM grads. I hired a young Masters grad from there to design a set. We rented the shop, and he built the set. Then I had to drive to Cincinnati to get it. To prevent throwing away sets, we rented a storage facility for $2,000 a year.

When asked how she felt about Hall Auditorium, the Miami Opera performance hall, she gave this response.

> Hall Auditorium is lacking as a facility for opera. As a concert hall, it is fine, but the renovation of the hall from 1991-93 did not address the needs of opera production. For one thing, there is only one dressing room for men and one for women.
>
> We have to be out of the hall at a certain time, or we have to pay overtime. The students put in a nine-hour day to load in the set. My husband and I would work a fourteen hour day. Then, at the end of the show the students have to take down the set and put it in storage. I found myself fund-raising to hire movers, so as not to exhaust the singers.
>
> I am excited about the future. We currently have collaboration with the Theatre Department. We tried for many years to do it. For many years, we all wanted to see it happen, but it meant faculty had to give up something to do it. This year, Theatre will do the set work and a director will be brought in. We now have a music theatre minor, which includes student vocal training. This collaboration may not be done every year. I am hopeful that this collaboration will be a fruitful one, so that Theatre feels that it gets help for its musicals and we get help for our operas.

GRAND NIGHT FOR SINGING

The year 2009 saw a new first-of-its-kind production at Miami, an evening of songs in the New York Broadway tradition. A review of this production stated that there were "songs from on and off Broadway...complete with soloists, small vocal ensembles, full chorus, a bit of dancing, full orchestra, a Broadway pianist, and full lighting and sound. The evening featured faculty, alumni, and 33 graduate and undergraduate students from across the MU campus." The review article continues with these words.

> The event brought several illustrious alumni back to campus as special soloists. Included in the lineup were countertenor William Sauerland (MU '04), Laura Smith (MU '99) and John Baldwin (MU '00), all of whom are having active careers within the profession.
>
> The three were featured in solo spots throughout the evening, Smith singing her signature operatic aria, 'Glitter and be Gay' from Bernstein's *Candide* and 'Somewhere Over the Rainbow' . . . Baldwin singing 'Being Alive' from *Company*, and Sauerland singing 'Crazy World' from *Victor, Victoria* and 'Smile' from *Modern Times*.
>
> Pianist Tedwin Blair Lindsay was featured in several solo pieces and accompanied the entire evening along with the orchestra. He proved to be a consummate professional with styles and technique well in hand. His solo version of 'Music of the Night' from *Phantom of the Opera* and 'Climb Every Mountain' from *Sound of Music* were cascades of technique and dash, reminiscent of Liberace.

This 'Grand Night' event became an annual event during the next four years, leading to new discussions within the Departments of Music and Theatre for establishing collaboration between the two departments in offering musical theatre productions. (See Mari Opatz-Muni's interview above.) For a list of Broadway musicals performed at Miami University under the direction of Dr. Jack Liles from 1980 to 2007, see Appendix D.

Chapter Thirteen

Music Faculty in Luxembourg and Echternach Festival Orchestra

Miami University established a study center in the Grand Duchy of Luxembourg in 1968. The program was set up to allow Miami students to spend a year abroad while continuing to earn degree credits for classes taken in Luxembourg. Miami faculty members were invited to submit proposals for Miami classes to be taught in the program, and native Luxembourg professors were hired to augment the number and variety of course offerings. Students were housed with local families near the City of Luxembourg where the study center was located. The center was initially named the Miami University European Center (MUEC) and later was renamed the Miami University Dolibois European Center (MUDEC) in honor of Ambassador John Dolibois who was instrumental in creating the study center. Ambassador Dolibois came to the United States from Luxembourg in his teens and received his undergraduate degree from Miami University, later to became Miami's Vice President for Alumni Affairs. MUDEC is still today one of Miami University's thriving foreign study programs.

Miami faculty who were appointed to teach at the European Center were expected to design courses with a strong relationship to Europe's culture past and present. One of their duties was to organize major field trips that took students to towns and cities in other countries as well as with Luxembourg itself. The first Miami music faculty member to be appointed as a professor and Visiting Scholar at the European Center was Joseph Bein, who taught chamber music repertoire and organized student attendance at live chamber music concerts in Luxembourg and the surrounding countries.

A second music faculty member, Jerome Stanley, was appointed to a similar position at the European Center in 1979. His course offering for the students was one in which music, art and architecture of Europe were combined and studied in the context of the major artistic periods of Western Europe. Dr. Stanley was appointed again for a two-year period, from 1987-1989, to teach the core course in the arts at the European Center. During those years, he organized class field trips to Bruges, Belgium; Cologne, Germany; Paris, France; and Vienna and Eisenstadt in Austria. Included on the trips were museums, lectures and concerts. In 1997, he taught the course there for a third and final time, organizing a class trip to Prague.

Other music faculty who contributed as Visiting Scholars to MUDEC during the 1990s were Professor Robert Thomas, performing a recital of classical works, and Professor John Heard, bassoonist, also performing a recital.

In the early 1980s, the curriculum at MUDEC added a course in music, now entitled *Great Ideas in Western Music,* which was taught for many years by faculty members residing in Luxembourg. Annie Hainsworth Lakos filled that position for several years. She offered *Great Ideas in Western Music* each fall term, and *Popular Concert Music* in the spring term. Music studied in class was made available to students on cassette tapes for study outside of class. She put a great deal of effort into making video-tapes from televised musical productions of classical music. She integrated student attendance at live concerts into her courses, thus taking advantage of the wealth of professional performances in Luxembourg. She designed her pre-concert lectures to explain the works to be performed. During field trips organized by other faculty in the social sciences, she served as the resource person for musical and other artistic events on the trips.

Georges Backes began teaching the course in 2000. He studied music at the Conservatory of Luxembourg, (First Prize Diploma), at the National Conservatory of Music in Stuttgart, Germany, at the Royal Conservatory of Brussels, Belgium (final diploma with "grande distinction") and at the Britten-Pears School for Advanced Musical Studies in Aldeburgh, Great-Britain. Formerly, he was a professor for voice training and "Lied" interpretation at the Music Conservatory in Luxembourg City, and he performed as a tenor with many orchestras all over Europe, with the conductors John Eliot Gardiner, Leopold Hager and others, performing oratorios and doing song recitals (*Liederabende*). He has also been a member of the Luxembourg National Music Council. His personal interests are the arts in general (music, painting, architecture) and travel. As of 2015, he was teaching the course *Great Ideas in Western Music* at MUDEC. In 2007, he began organizing study tours for his classes. Between 2007 and 2011, these tours included each semester one tour of Germany, Austria or Italy. The topics and cities were as follows:

Germany: In the Tracks of Johann Sebastian Bach—Eisenach/Weimar/ Leipzig
Austria: The City of Vienna in Music History

Italy: Venice, Cradle of Baroque Music
Germany: Famous German Composers in Eisenach/Weimar/Leipzig/Dresden
Italy: In the Tracks of Rossini, Verdi and Puccini
Pesaro/Busseto/Lucca/Torre del Lago/Milan

Between 2012 and 2015, additional tours were added:

Germany:"In the Tracks of Important German Composers Around Bach and Handel—Eisenach/Weimar/Halle/Leipzig
Austria: Vienna, Great City of the Great Composers
Great Britain: Benjamin Britten's Centenary Festivities in Aldeburgh

More recently, Professors Andrea Ridilla and Thomas Garcia taught at the European Center. During an interview with Professor Ridilla, she made the following comments, revealing how the Luxembourg teaching experience enriched her career.

> A recent development for me has been teaching at the Miami University Dolibois European Center in Luxembourg, Miami's European campus. I had a Summer Professorship there in 2011 and 2013. In Summer 2011, part of my course, "Opera: Passport to the Liberal Arts," involved taking the students to performances of the operetta, "The Merry Widow," in Vienna and an avant-garde production of Richard Strauss' Salome at the Komische Oper Berlin. A Miami Plan course, it is aimed at the general liberal arts student many of whom have had no prior musical training, or coursework in music. The experience opens the door to a new world for lifelong exploration. In Summer 2013, I took the students to see Verdi's Aida at the Arena of Verona and Richard Wagner's *Das Rheingold* from the Ring Cycle at La Scala Opera House in Milan, Italy.

Professor Garcia, Associate Professor of Ethnomusicology and Latin American Studies, taught two courses at the Center: one on African-American Music in Europe, and another on European Folk, Popular and Classical Music.

ECHTERNACH FESTIVAL ORCHESTRA

In the late 1980s, an idea developed for having Miami faculty and student performers join with musicians in Luxembourg to form the orchestra for the annual International Music Festival in the city of Echternach, Luxembourg. This festival is scheduled in the early part of each summer and features internationally renowned soloists and groups that perform with the orchestra in a two-week series of concerts. The creation of this collaboration between

Miami and Luxembourg was a unique opportunity to showcase Miami musicians and to have them represent the United States as musical ambassadors.

Department Chair John Heard and Miami Symphony Orchestra Conductor Carmon DeLeone were invited to a meeting in Luxembourg with officials of the Luxembourg Conservatory of Music and the Echternach Festival Board of Directors to discuss details for drawing up an agreement for the Festival Orchestra.

In a 2013 interview, John Heard gave the following information about the creation of the Miami/Luxembourg student/faculty musician exchange:

> Through dialogue with the Board of Directors of the Festival International Echternach, it was determined that Miami music professors and selected Miami music students, along with a similar contingent from the Luxembourg Conservatory of Music, would perform in the annual Echternach Festival Orchestra conducted by the Miami University Symphony Orchestra conductor, Carmon DeLeone. This created further opportunities for performances in Germany, France, and Belgium. At the same time (1991-2001), an agreement between Miami's Music Department and the Luxembourg Conservatory of Music created an international student/faculty exchange.
>
> During these years of Miami faculty and student participation in the Festival, commendations were sent to the Department from the Governor of Ohio,

Echternach Festival Orchestra. Photograph courtesy of Echternach Fesitval.

the Grand Duke of Luxembourg, the American Ambassador to Luxembourg, the Mayor of Luxembourg, and the European Parliament. In addition, the musicians were given favorable reviews in major European newspapers and broadcasts over radio and television.

The beneficial affiliation of Miami University faculty and students with the Echternach Festival Orchestra lasted from 1999 to 2006. It had been established under the Department Chair John Heard in 1999. Much to the dismay of the Department, the University discontinued the funding for this opportunity in 2006. It had been a unique international experience for faculty and students. One music faculty member, who had been a student in Salzburg, had a connection with a Salzburg conductor, Yoon K. Lee. When Mr. Lee was contracted to form an orchestra for a CD recording with pianist Cyprian Katsaris performing Bach concerti, he invited the Miami string faculty and one student to join other European musicians for that project. This opportunity occurred as the result of the Echternach connection.

After the demise of the annual Festival project, music faculty members expressed how much they missed having that yearly experience. It was a widely recognized European music festival that regularly attracted major solo performers and opera artists. At the time, there was a Venezuelan graduate student string quartet at Miami, and they performed and were reviewed in Germany because of the Echternach connection. The Festival was a good recruiting tool. It was an international opportunity for the Department that no longer exists.

Oboe Professor Andrea Ridilla was a faculty member who gained valuable experience by performing in the Luxembourg Echternach Festival Orchestra. Through her connection with the ensemble she was able to give her students performing opportunities in the orchestra as well. She comments:

> The Echternach Festival Orchestra program in Luxembourg, in which the Department of Music collaborated from 1999–2005, was my best recruitment tool. Private teachers recommended students to Miami for the international performance experience they would get in Europe during their undergraduate studies. After the demise of the Echternach program, however, it became more difficult to recruit.

John Heard, during his years as Chair of the Department of Music, established some very beneficial additions to the music curriculum that allowed for a wider range of chamber music experiences for both students and faculty. His 2013 interview, found in Appendix E, outlines these projects.

Chapter Fourteen

Dreams Come True

The Miami University Department of Music is proud of a history in which its faculty has given countless hours of attention to student progress beyond the normal expectations of faculty. Chapter Four above included information about a voice student, Bes-Arlene Crase, who realized her dream of entering the world of musical performance. Such student dreams can come true only when the right environment is supplied. Miami's Department of Music has had a history of providing such an environment.

In the late 1970s and into the 80s, the Ohio Board of Regents and the State Legislature began to question what was considered to be a proliferation of academic programs in Ohio higher education. For example, Miami's Department of Music being geographically so near Cincinnati's College-Conservatory of Music caused a questioning of the role of Miami's music program in relation to Cincinnati and other Ohio universities.

The argument must be put forth that all students seeking a music education in Ohio deserve equal opportunity at any and all of the State's universities. When a student enters an institution as a freshman, there is no way of knowing how that student's talent will develop. Every institution should be equipped to provide the right environment and high quality faculty to insure that talented students receive the best possible education.

There are many success stories of music alumni who have brought honor to Miami University through their high professional achievements. Their comments about the quality of Miami's Department of Music continue to raise public awareness leading to recruitment of excellent students who come to the University with their own high expectations of achievement.

James Miltenberger, pianist, became a Professor of Music at the University of West Virginia. He was a native of Sydney, Ohio, and received his baccalaureate degree from Miami University in 1960. He graduated with his master's and doctoral degrees from the Eastman School of Music at the University of Rochester. Thereafter, with some consideration of suggestions he had received from former West Virginia University music theory professor Frank Lawrence, Miltenberger and his wife moved to Morgantown. He was one among the first group of faculty there to be named a West Virginia University Foundation Outstanding teacher. He has performed extensively as a soloist nationally as well as in Europe and Japan, including appearances at Carnegie Hall and with the Pittsburgh Symphony Orchestra. He has had nationwide television appearances on PBS and the NBC Today Show.

David Meeker, music educator, earned a Bachelor of Science degree in education from Miami University in 1956, a Master of Music degree from the University of Michigan, and a PhD degree from Kent State University. He taught music at public high schools in Bucyrus, Akron and Warrensville Heights, Ohio. From 1968 to 1977, he was an associate professor in music education and later a full professor at Ohio State University.

Harold Weller, the founder and conductor of the Las Vegas Philharmonic Orchestra who retired in 2008, studied music at Miami from 1964-1970. The author's lengthy phone interview with Mr. Weller in 2013 touched upon some important ideas concerning music education in America. His interest in young musicians inspired his involvement with a Las Vegas foundation to help inner city children called 'Violins for Kids.'

Using as an example the renowned approach to music for youth in Venezuela known as *El Systema*, founded in 1975 by José Antonio Abreu, Mr. Weller discussed how such a program taps into the very heart of music-making. *El Systema* is a publicly financed voluntary music education program that was originally called by its founder *Social Action for Music*. This social action approach distinguishes it from the more conventional way of introducing youth to music through public school education. Ideas that surfaced during the conversation hinted at the possibility that a conventional public school atmosphere might not offer the student sufficient freedom to jump headlong into the world of music-making with a sense of personal freedom. Here is a portion of the interview with Mr. Weller.

> I have always been interested in young people. I went to Interlochen for two summers. In Hamilton, Ohio, we formed the Butler County Youth Orchestra. I have always championed young budding artists.
>
> The smartness of the *El Systema* is that it is a social welfare program as opposed to an artsy approach to music. I was once at Disney Hall in L.A. when the *El Systema* orchestra performed the Mahler Symphony No. Five and Stravinsky's Petroushka. During the evening, a door at the side of the hall opened, and José Abreu came in, like a saint coming into the hall. I've never experienced such passion in musicians before.

As the interview with Mr. Weller continued, he told how his life progressed from his student days at Miami to his final position as Conductor of the Las Vegas Philharmonic Orchestra.

> When I was at Miami University, I was a horrible student. But Joe Bein knew that I wanted to be a conductor, and he facilitated my becoming the Assistant Conductor of the Dayton Philharmonic Orchestra.
> In 1970, I went to Ashland College in Ohio as an Instructor, and there I formed an orchestra. In the second year it was a seventy-piece orchestra. Then, I moved on to Old Dominion in Virginia in 1977 and started an orchestra there. In 1979, I went to the University of New Mexico as Assistant Conductor. In the early 80s I was judging a competition when I ran into someone who was looking for someone to take the conducting post with the Flagstaff Symphony. I accepted the job there as both Conductor and Manager. During my fifteen years at Flagstaff, I increased the season to twenty-two concerts per year and developed their endowment from zero to over a million dollars.
> In 1997, the Nevada Symphony was in financial trouble and had to go out of business. I was called to Las Vegas in late June of that year and asked to form a new orchestra known as the Las Vegas Philharmonic. I remained Conductor of that orchestra from 1997 until my retirement in 2008.

Sam Pellman, composer, attended Miami University from 1971 to 1975. After receiving the Master of Music and the doctorate from Cornell University, he took a position at Hamilton College in Clinton, New York, where he served as Chair of the Music Department. Many of his works may be heard on recordings by the Musical Heritage Society. Much of his music is published by the Continental Music Press and Wesleyan Music Press. His music has recently been presented at festivals and conferences in Melbourne, Paris, Basel, Vienna, Montreal, New York City, Bejing, Capetown, Taiwan, Perth , and Buenos Aires. Pellman is also the author of *An Introduction to the Creation of Electroacoustic Music,* a widely-adopted textbook published by Cengage. At Hamilton College he teaches theory and composition and is co-director of the Studio for Transmedia Arts and Related Studies. Speaking during an interview, Dr. Pellman related the following thoughts about his training, career and views on music education.

> David Cope was a major influence on me, as was Anne Baxter. In my work with Ms. Baxter, I studied the Beethoven 'Tempest' sonata as well as Opus 109. My studies with these faculty members allowed the valuable one-on-one relationship.
> Academic institutions tend to focus on research, but in the case of conductors and composers, the emphasis must be on practice. Thus, the 'research' for a faculty string quartet, for example, is the practice and performance of the great works belonging to that repertoire.
> Hamilton College, where I'm a member of the faculty, built a music performance hall twenty-five years ago. And now they are building a new arts

building. The Dean thought that I would have insights on this current building project since I was among the planners for the music hall. Among the architects that we reviewed for the job was one who had done a study a Miami University and had included a rendering of the music auditorium that was designed for Miami but never built.

David Felder, composer, did his undergraduate work in music at Miami University from 1971-75. He received his PhD in music from The University of California at San Diego. He has been described as "a Gustav Mahler for the twenty-first century. As of 2013, he is Distinguished Professor at SUNY Buffalo, New York, and Birge-Cary Chair in Music Composition there. He has received numerous grants and commissions including many awards from the National Endowment for the Arts, two New York State Council commissions, a New York Foundation for the Arts Fellowship, Guggenheim award, two Koussevitzky commissions, two Fromm Foundation Fellowships, two awards from the Rockefeller Foundation, and many more.

In a 2013 interview, he offered many thoughts about his undergraduate experience at Miami and about the status of American university music programs in the twenty-first century.

> I often give full credit to my years at Miami that allowed me to become what I am today. My experience at Miami allowed me to enter the path that led me to where I am today. I entered Miami as a freshman with the idea of being a high school choral conductor. My public school years in Cleveland gave me the opportunity to sing in the Cleveland Orchestra Chorus. I had ear-training and harmony lessons with a woman who worked as piano accompanist in the Cleveland Orchestra. Pierre Boulez was the orchestra conductor there at the time.
>
> When I came to Miami, I never thought of the possibility of becoming a composer. But, the faculty members helped to change my mind. I had classes with theorist Joseph Bein and composer David Cope, and my work with them brought about a big change in my thinking. The Department faculty were great, a bunch of professors willing to engage with students. It was a propitious moment. Dr. Paul Aliapoulios had come to Miami as Chair of the Department of Music. A very influential faculty member for me was 'Jocko' Cummings. He took a strong liking to me, and I would meet with him in his home for analysis projects. He would assign me some well-known composition and say "Why is every note there?" He had me use a Walter Piston system for analysis. It was amazing. I would complete 60 or 70 hand-written pages of analysis on one project.
>
> While at Miami, there was an ensemble called the Ensemble for New Music that had an influence on me. Also, the Department purchased synthesizers for use in the electronic lab. I began to focus on composition as my musical direction.
>
> After my graduation from Miami, composer Donald Erb hired me for a year, 1978-79, to teach electronic music at the Cleveland Institute of Music, where there was also a Saturday program for ear-training and harmony study.

Concerning his thoughts about music in higher education, Felder offered his professional insight based upon experience.

> I've had a lot of experience in different music programs and administrative work. Today, there are many challenges in trying to deal with university administrators to advocate the needs of music in higher education.
>
> A big problem with university music programs is their expense, largely due to the need to teach private applied music instruction at a time when universities are moving toward online instruction. There is now an online music instruction program using 'Skype.' Administrators want to know why we do not want to teach music that way. We need to make a convincing case as to why we want small classes and individual tutorials. Many musicians have not learned why it's important to teach this way, and therefore they do not make convincing advocates.
>
> A second obstacle in university music departments is the problem of heavy student course loads, mandated by the state, for music education majors. I feel that many of these education courses are unnecessary. They are a drain on the resources of faculty and students. The in-house political tensions and budget strife between music education faculty and performance faculty causes a lot of bickering. Everyone is striving to get budget dollars for their own areas. Added to those faculty members are other faculty in the areas of music theory and musicology. A lot of musicians are opinionated, so they do not pull together to work toward a broader agenda. We need to find a better way internally to advocate our needs to the upper administration. University administrators are mainly aware of the glee club or the band on the football field, but are not as much aware of other important aspects of a music program.

In the interview, Felder was asked about his career experiences and his reasons for staying many years at SUNY Buffalo. He says, "At Buffalo I have a unique situation that I like. I had an offer for a faculty position at Harvard, but I turned it down. At SUNY Buffalo I have my own chamber orchestra with about five concerts a year and a budget of about $350,000 a year."

David Bell, composer, did his undergraduate work at Miami University in the early 1970s and received a Master's Degree from the Eastman School of Music in 1977. From 1984 to 1991 he contributed music to seventy-nine TV episodes of *Murder, She Wrote;* five episodes of *Dr. Quin, Medicine Woman*; followed by sixty-six episodes of Star Trek shows from 1994 to 2003. In 2002 he won the ASCAP Award (Top TV Series) for *Enterprise* shared with the series' other regular composers. He is also the author of *Getting the Best Score for Your Film*, a book that was highly praised for its clear, sharp writing and comprehensive study of the subject. In his own words from the book, when asked how he became a successful composer, he responded:

> It was a gradual thing that evolved over many years, very often involving detours, flexibility of plans, a process of trying many things and eliminating

certain things that didn't work well for me. I had dabbled with arranging in high school and learned that I had a pretty good ear, especially for orchestration. I don't play keyboard very well, but was a pretty fair trumpet player and conductor. However, when working on my undergraduate degree at Miami U of Ohio, I gradually realized that I enjoyed creating works as a composer as well as re-creating works others had written as a performer and conductor.

Gary Holt enjoyed a career as Professor of Music at the *Hochschule für Musik* in Cologne, Germany. He received the degrees Bachelor of Music and Master of Music, both in cello performance, from Miami University under Professor Potteiger. After leaving Miami he studied privately in London and matriculated as a student at the *Hochschule für Musik und Tanz* in Cologne, Germany. He joined the faculty there in 1980 and was still a member of that faculty in 2013. In 2003, the *Hochschule* appointed him Honorary Professor. In a message to the author in the spring of 2013, he speaks about his cello professor at Miami, Elizabeth Potteiger. (See also his interview in Appendix E.)

> When I think about Liz, I feel that she made a better person out of every student who had the fortune to have met and studied with her. She was so dedicated to each and every one of us. We were all treated equally and if a little bit of immaturity on our part appeared, we were very quickly and firmly corrected. She helped us become responsible and caring adults.
>
> I feel very strongly about Liz and what a wonderful influence she had on us. You know, the two of us met so many times after I graduated. At first it was usually in London and we spent days together, usually going to a play, an opera or a ballet every day. Every free minute we had was spent talking to each other. Later I came to Oxford as often as possible and we would pick up where we left off. Even though I ended up playing the piano, it was Liz who somehow got me on the right track with cello, then gamba and eventually Europe. We had a wonderful relationship.

Christina Carr, mezzo soprano, is a graduate of Miami University with a Bachelor of Music in Performance from the Eastman School of Music and a Master's of Music in Performance and Literature. She is an aluma of the Juilliard Opera Center with an Artist Diploma. Following her time at Juilliard, she was an apprentice artist at Central City Opera where she premiered the role of Janie in Mollicon's *Gabriel's Daughter* and Zulma in Rossini's *L'Italiana in Algeri*. She has performed leading operatic roles in Verdi's *Rigoletto, Il Trovatore* and *Aida;* Wagner's *Tannhäuser, Tristan und Isolde, Parsifal,* and *Die Walküre;* and in a number of other operas by Puccini, Donizetti and Rosinni. She is also an active recitalist and concert soloist.

At Miami University, Ms. Carr was a prizewinner of the Miami Concerto Competition, and during those undergraduate years she was also a member of the Cincinnati Opera professional opera chorus. At Eastman School of Music, she performed a variety of leading roles, including Handel's *Xerxes*, Gilbert & Sullivan's *Patience*, and Vaughan William's *Riders to the Sea*. She won second place in the Lotte Lenya competition, third and second place in the Eastman Lieder competition two consecutive years, and was a district finalist in the Metropolitan Opera Council Competition. At the Juilliard Opera Center, she performed roles in Floyd's *Susannah*, Poulenc's *Dialogues of the Carmelites*, and Paulus's *Heloise and Abelard*. She has worked with Opera Omaha, Taconic Opera, Opera Circle, Garden State Opera, Cincinnati Opera and the Wagner Intensive, among others.

Steven Reineke is a Miami music alumnus who graduated with degrees in music performance and composition. He was awarded the Joanna Jackson Goldman Memorial Prize that enabled him to go, immediately upon graduation, to Los Angeles for private studies with professional music composers and arrangers. Following those studies, he returned to Ohio to become the protégé of Erich Kunzel, Director of the Cincinnati Pops Orchestra, a position that he held for the next several years.

Steven Reineke started his tenure as Music Director of The New York Pops in the 2009-2010 season. Mr. Reineke conducts the orchestra's annual concert series at Carnegie Hall as well as tours, recordings, and nationwide telecasts, including the Macy's 4th of July Fireworks Spectacular on NBC Television. New York's only permanent and professional symphonic pops orchestra, The New York Pops is the largest independent pops orchestra in the United States.

During the 2011-2012 season, Reineke was appointed Principal Pops Conductor of the National Symphony Orchestra; during the 2012-2013 season, he was appointed the Principal Pops Conductor of the Toronto Symphony Orchestra. He previously served as Principal Pops Conductor of the Long Beach and Modesto Symphony Orchestras. He was also Associate Conductor of the Cincinnati Pops Orchestra, where for fifteen years he served as a composer, arranger and conducting protégé of the late celebrated pops conductor Erich Kunzel.

In 2009 he made his Boston Pops and Philadelphia Orchestra débuts, and made his Asian début conducting the National Taiwan Symphony Orchestra. In 2008 Mr. Reineke made his Carnegie Hall début conducting The New York Pops 25th Birthday Gala. He made his Hollywood Bowl début in 2007 with the multi-faceted entertainer Wayne Brady and returned to the Hollywood Bowl in 2008 to conduct the Los Angeles Philharmonic. In addition, Reineke conducted, arranged and orchestrated the music for Brady's orchestral show and played the same role in his collaboration with rock legend Peter Frampton. An interview in 2013 with Mr. Reineke tells his story in his own words:

Steven Reineke, photo by Michael Tammaro.

Coming to Miami University as a young trumpet player I didn't know what to expect. I had auditioned at the Eastman School and really wanted to go there, but I didn't get in. I received a scholarship at Miami and fell in love with it. There was an intense environment there, and the opportunities were so great. There were so many wonderful teachers with true interest in their students, and I had complete freedom and flexibility in creating my own program. I had a lot of one-on-one time with my professors, taking independent studies in areas like conducting.

Professor Harvey Stokes had a huge influence on my composing and arranging. He gave me a list of probably 150 important classical works and told me to get the scores from the library and learn about them. Dr. James Sheppard and Roger Davis also worked with me one-on-one. Their influence was in contemporary and commercial music.

At Miami, I was so fortunate to have my compositions performed immediately after finishing them. It was a dream situation, like being an architect and having my creations immediately brought to life. At other institutions, especially larger ones, there would not have been that opportunity. So often I have talked with students who studied at other schools, and they cannot believe how lucky I was. They would say, 'Are you kidding, you get your pieces played as soon as you write them?'

Other influences on me at Miami were Carmon DeLeone, conductor of the Cincinnati Ballet, and Gary Speck, who had just been appointed to the music faculty in 1988. Also, Ron Matson was a faculty member who had one of the strongest musical influences on me. He was the piano accompanist in my trumpet performances, but beyond that he discovered that when I hear music, I see what it looks like on the page. That was an earth-shattering event for me. Ron told me that it was a gift and that I had a responsibility to use it.

When I won the Goldman prize at graduation, I packed up my car and went to LA to study privately with different professional musicians. Carmon DeLeone asked me to come back to Cincinnati to orchestrate the 90-minute ballet, *Peter Pan*. That brought me to the attention of Erich Kunzel, director of the Cincinnati Pops Orchestra. I was in Cincinnati for several years and then moved to New York in September 2009. Now I'm trying to balance composing/arranging with conducting. The conducting career has taken off just recently.

The above interview concluded with Mr. Reineke's words, "I love what I'm doing." This story gives a perfect illustration of how a young student entered Miami and was inspired by his professors to map out a course for himself as a musician that ultimately brought him to a prime position as one of America's sought-after musical personalities.

Chapter Fifteen

University Artists Series and Department Residencies

One might say that observations about twenty-first-century society indicate a lower level of citizens' involvement in the European classical music tradition and modern concert-hall music in general. Such writers as American composer Ned Rorem have been suggesting this as a prevalent condition. The difficulties of survival that many orchestras and other musical organizations have encountered seem to support that assessment. The former ways in which classical music recordings were distributed via large store outlets have given way to online purchasing. The absence of those stores prevent any immediate impression of how well or how poorly classical music albums are selling. But, the decline in such sales that were seen in the music sections of large chain book stores from the 1970s through the 90s would suggest that sales of classical albums was in sharp decline at the turn of the present century.

Music education in this country has attempted to expose children and young adults to the best possible musical experiences during their public school years. But, as everyone knows, the first school instructional programs to be cut during any budget crisis are the music and art programs. This happens in spite of research indicating the importance of music education, for example. According to the Florida Music Educators Association:

> Music and the Fine Arts have been a significant portion of every culture's educational system for more than 3,000 years. The human brain has been shown to be "hard-wired" for music; there is a biological basis for music being an important part of human experience. Music and the Arts surround daily life in our present day culture. Most present day artists, architects, and musicians acquired their interests during public school Fine Arts classes... Education

without the Fine Arts is fundamentally impoverished and subsequently leads to an impoverished society.

The advantage of live musical performance versus recorded music has long been observed. Live music is a process by which listeners share deep emotional experiences with others. The mystery of this process has long been a source of inspiration to those who share the experience. Dr. Myers referred to this in his statement printed in the May, 1906 issue of *The Miami Recensio*.

> It is recognized that as literature represents the best poetic and dramatic thought of the past and present, so music represents the highest genius and the best social, moral and religious thought in the history of the development of the human race and is, therefore, an inheritance of value equal to any art or science in our educational system.

As pointed out in Chapter Two above, there was already a 'Liceum Course' in existence at Miami University at the turn of the twentieth century that was designed to bring outside lecturers and musicians for the benefit of the community and its students. It served the combined student population of Oxford College, Western College for Women, and Miami University. As time moved on, this type of offering continued until the separation of a lecture series from the musical Artists Series. The *Benton Bulletin* offered the following history of Miami's early Lyceum offerings:

> The editor of the Benton Bulletin thought that a brief survey of the early endeavors of the University to provide public entertainment for the students of Oxford College, Western, and Miami might be at least of historic interest.
>
> As soon as Benton Auditorium [now Hall Auditorium] became available, the demand for a more and varied public entertainment was made... The total student body in the three colleges was less than 1,000 at the opening of the course, with the policy of only four entertainments for the season but of the most eminent. Of the eight orchestras, Russian Royal, St. Louis, Cleveland, Detroit, Cincinnati, Dresden Royal, New York Symphony, the London Symphony were most notable. The Detroit's conductor was Garbilovitch, himself a distinguished pianist and husband of Mark Twain's daughter... On the Gabrilovitch program, one of Dr. Edgar Stillman Kelley's scores for orchestra...was given. Dr. Kelley at the time was accredited by Musical America magazine to be the greatest living American composer...
>
> The New York Symphony with conductor Walter Damrosch, founder and at the time a most popular conductor, and George Barrer, world's greatest flutist, gave one or two numbers with encores...
>
> The London Symphony was an accidental catch, a result of exact timing . . . The announcement of the conductor's name alone was sufficient to create interest next to excitement among music lovers and critics. Mr. Nikisch was at the time the world's greatest master of the baton, 57 years of age,

member of Wagner's Symphony in Bayreuth, conductor of leading symphonies of Europe, of Boston Symphony 1889-93, for some years conductor of the London Symphony. Like Toscanini, he conducted whole programs without the score. The auditorium was crowded with guests from Cincinnati Hamilton, and other adjacent cities.

By 1950, Professor Henry C. Montgomery, of the Classics Department, had become the Director of the Artists Series. In addition to the Artists Series for the regular academic year, in the 1950s and 1960s there was an additional Summer Artists Series that also featured classical artists of international renown. A newspaper article of the time reported the high quality of the Artists Series at Miami University:

> Few universities in the country, regardless of size can boast of an Artists Series program as diverse and as extensive as that presented here through the efforts of Prof. Henry C. Montgomery . . .
>
> Many of the most prominent names in contemporary American music have...appeared before the Miami student body, including Alec Templeton, Artur Rubenstein, Helen Traubel, Rise Stevens, Jan Peerce, Jascha Heifetz, Jose Iturbi, Lauritz Melchior, Marian Anderson and Zino Francescatti . . .
>
> Visitors have been known to come from 1,000 miles away to hear an artist play a certain selection.

The Artists Series for the season 1955-56 included the Cincinnati Symphony Orchestra; Robert Merrill, baritone; The Vienna Choir Boys; Jorge Bolet, pianist; Cesare Valletti, tenor; and Irmgard Seefried, soprano. The 1957-58 season featured, among others, Roberta Peters, soprano; The New York Woodwind Quintet; and Andres Segovia, classical guitarist. In 1961, Ravi Shankar performed a program of sitar music. In 1965, the famed tenor Nicolai Gedda performed on the Series.

The Series for 1973-74 included the following artists: Julian Bream, guitarist and lutenist; Maureen Forrester, contralto; Jacques Klein, pianist; Goldovsky Grand Opera Theatre; Denver Symphony Orchestra, Cincinnati Ballet Company; and Edith Peinemann, violinist. For 1974-75, the roster included Agnes de Mille Heritage Dance Theater; Leipzig Gewandhaus Orchestra; Justino Diaz, basso; Gerre Hancock, organist; Tokyo String Quartet; and Rebecca Penneys, pianist.

The headline of a front-page article appearing in the November 21st, 1975 issue of *The Miami Student* reads "Soviet pianist debut in U.S. to be here." The pianist was Lazar Berman. Beneath his photo accompanying the article was the caption "Lazar Berman will make his United States debut at a Miami Artists Series concert." The article goes on to give the following account.

Artist Series is sponsoring Berman's appearance here, and Chairman David Bean negotiated this coup for Miami through his own manager, Jacques Leiser.

Leiser signed the contract with Berman and the Soviet agency regulating foreign tours last March. He "traded" Berman for Bean, also a concert pianist, who will make an exchange tour in the Soviet Union in the fall of 1977 . . .

Berman, 45, has been with the Moscow Philharmonic for more than 17 years, but has only toured outside his country in Eastern Europe and Italy . . .

Bean said Miami would hold a press conference for Berman. Berman does not speak English, so an interpreter will accompany him on his trip, Bean added.

Both President Phillip Shriver and Bean will be inviting VIP's from various schools and the arts to attend the conference. Bean said he will be taking an ad in the Sunday, Dec. 14, issue of The New York Times to draw attention to the unusual debut.

Russian pianist Lazar Berman with interpreter Josette Thévenin-Stanley. Image provided by Miami University Libraries, Oxford, OH.

The American debut recital of pianist Lazar Berman took place in Millet Hall on January 14th, 1976. Mr. Berman's Miami appearance was co-sponsored by the Miami University Artists Series and the Ohio Arts Council. His Miami appearance drew national attention and was the subject of an interview with

Berman in *High Fidelity* magazine written by Barry James and Vadim Yurchenkov. An Associated Press article at the time summed up Berman's catapult to fame: "Pianist Lazar Berman has moved rapidly from the status of one of the world's best-kept secrets to superstardom. He often is compared with Vladimir Horowitz, both for the dazzling pianism and for his ability to sell out concert halls overnight."

DEPARTMENTAL RESIDENCIES

A great university has the responsibility of preserving the arts through public presentation of significant artists. The Miami University Artists Series (renamed in 1987 the Performing Arts Series) was one means of achieving this goal. Another way in which historically significant music was presented at Miami was through the many artists brought to the campus by the Department of Music. As the Department of Music gained strength and financial support into the mid-twentieth century, it was able to host residencies and special appearances of many performing artists and composers. Over the years there were many such residencies, and the following are but a few examples.

PIANIST ROBERT GOLDSAND

During the 1950s and into the 1960s, world-renowned pianist Robert Goldsand came from his faculty position at Manhattan School of Music in New York City to give piano workshops at Miami University. The *New York Herald–Tribune* wrote that he was "among the foremost of our contemporary pianists, both as technician and as interpreter."

COMPOSER AARON COPLAND

The Miami Student newspaper issue of April 6, 1976, reported a New Music Festival that coincided with the American Bicentennial. The festival featured the residency of American composer Aaron Copland. Mr. Copland gave a public lecture and was honored with performances of many of his works. Students and faculty of the Department of Music participated in these concerts. Musicians and ensembles among the performances included the Miami Symphony Orchestra, the A Cappella Singers, the Miami Wind Ensemble, the Miami Ensemble for New Music, and various soloists and small instrumental ensembles.

Miami's resident composer at the time, David Cope, made the arrangements for Mr. Copland's ten-day appearance and did the organizing of performers for three programs of Copland's works and a public lecture during the residency. Venues for the various events were Hall Auditorium, Souers Recital Hall, and Millett Hall. David Cope recalls his experience in this landmark event on Miami's campus.

> I spent ten days with Aaron Copland during the early spring of 1976 at Miami University of Ohio. This represented a remarkable opportunity for me, since Copland had been a major influence on my life and music since my early childhood. During these ten days I served primarily as his chauffeur, guide, confidant, and gofer. Copland was in his late seventies at the time and I in my middle forties. Yet it was I who often found myself exhausted and unable to keep up with his seemingly tireless energy.
>
> I discovered the source of at least some of Copland's energy when he prepared for and conducted the concert of his music during his visit. Even when rehearsing for this concert, it was clear that he had mastered the art of energy conservation. In fact, often during breaks in rehearsals or between pieces at the resulting concert, he would collapse in the nearest chair and immediately fall asleep. I got used to waking him at the last minute, watching him struggle out of his chair, only to see him tap some unseen energy source that would then literally propel him onto the podium.
>
> Copland's ability to instantly relax was most notably apparent after the final piece of the concert, his Fanfare for the Common Man. He wielded his baton extraordinarily throughout this work, and the concert concluded with a professional fireworks show, the likes of which I have yet to see repeated. Copland never saw these fireworks. As soon as the audience turned away from the stage toward the magic of the lights, Copland narcoleptically swan-dived into the nearest chair and once again fell deeply asleep.

COMPOSER SYLVIE BODOROVA

The School of Fine Arts and Department of Music sponsored the residency of composer Sylvie Bodorova, a native of Prague, Czechoslovakia, in 1993. Her residency was made possible by grants from Sigma Chi/William P. Huffman Scholars in Residence and from Meet the Composer, Inc., with additional support from the National Endowment for the Arts and the Dayton Hudson Foundation.

An article and photograph of Ms. Bodorova in the *Miami Student* of March 5th, 1993, announced her appearance and a concert of her music.

> The concert has been organized in conjunction with the week-long program, "Women in Music 1993," sponsored by the Miami University School of Fine Arts and the Department of Music. Bodorova will be the Composer in Residence with the School of Fine Arts throughout the week in her first visit to the United States.

Chapter Sixteen

The Larger Community

As outlined in the Introduction, this history focuses on the development of Miami University's Department of Music. However, for many years the small community of Oxford, Ohio, was the scene of not one, but two separate schools each having its own Music Department. A discussion of music at Miami would not be complete without due reference to the Music Department at the Western College for Women. This private college opened in 1853 and closed in 1974. Miami University purchased the campus, and it became the Western College of Miami University.

In 1916, the graduating class of the Western College for Women raised funds to build a home and studio, referred to as the Kelley Cottage, for the first composer artist-in-residence ever appointed to a college campus. The structure still stands at its original site. In the spring of 2015, the University administration was interested in a plan to demolish the building in order to use the site for a new student dormitory. But, the cottage escaped that fate. The Chair of the Department of Music at that time, Bruce Murray, tried in vain to convince the administration to allow the Department use of the building. Since it had been created as a composer's home and studio, this seemed a logical suggestion. The composer was Edgar Stillman Kelley (1857–1944). The Western Archives at Miami University gives this synopsis of his musical training and career:

> Kelley graduated from the Stuttgart Conservatory in 1880 and performed widely in Europe with world-class orchestras. Returning to the U.S., he settled in San Francisco, went to work as a church organist, and wrote music reviews for the Examiner. National acclaim as a composer came with the orchestral score for a production of Macbeth. Kelley's love of Asian culture is evident in the brilliant Aladdin Suite. Both these pieces are still widely performed before American and European audiences.

In 1910, Edgar Stillman Kelley was already enjoying a distinguished career in the U.S. and abroad when his wife, Jessie, accepted a position as director of piano music at Western College for Women. Kelley was given a fellowship, which would allow him the freedom to concentrate on his composition, and he thereby became the first creative artist-in-residence at an American college or university. It was here that Kelley wrote his first book, *Chopin the Composer*, published in 1913, and composed two of his finest works, the *New England Symphony* and the oratorio *Pilgrim's Progress*.

Edgar Stillman Kelley is recognized as the quintessential American composer of the early 20th century. Widely regarded also as a pianist, conductor, scholar, teacher, lecturer and author, he produced music that captured the hearts and minds of audiences and music critics. Kelley endeavored to express in his music all that is true and fine in classical music traditions - but with a spirit of adventure and enterprise, as well.

Edgar Stillman Kelley was beloved by the students and faculty at Western College and produced many of his best works here. The Kelleys lived busy lives in Oxford, dividing their time between Western and the Cincinnati Conservatory of Music, where "Dr. Kelley" taught composition and "Mrs. Kelley" lectured. After retirement in 1934, the couple continued to travel—conducting and performing Kelley's music for the world but returning for a few months each year to the little studio cottage that had been built for them on the Western campus. Edgar Stillman Kelley died on November 12, 1944.

Precisely at the same time when Miami's School of Fine Arts was established in 1929, the Theodore Presser Foundation supported the construction of Presser Hall on the Western campus that was designed specifically as a music facility. The building was completed in 1931. The Presser Foundation website gives this overview:

> The Presser Foundation was established in 1939 under the Deeds of Trust and Will of the late Theodore Presser (1848–1925), an educator, publisher and philanthropist. It is one of the few private foundations in the United States dedicated solely to music education and music philanthropy.

Western College for Women closed in 1974, and the campus was purchased by Miami University. For many years the building was used by various departments as a classroom building. It was not until 2008 that the building was renovated for sole use by Miami's Department of Music. Some critics of the renovation cited the loss of the original auditorium with its good acoustics and suitability for chamber music. The renovation called for the old auditorium to become a two-floor unit partitioned into separate spaces.

The Miami University website gives this history of Presser Hall:

> Presser Hall is named for the renowned music publisher Theodore Presser and for the foundation that bears his name. The Presser Foundation provided vital support for the construction of the building, which opened in 1931. In 2008

Presser Hall was expanded and renovated thoroughly. Today it contains classrooms, rehearsal rooms, practice rooms, faculty studios and offices, libraries for band, choral, and orchestral music, and the Department of Music Office. Presser Hall also contains several rooms with special purposes and equipment, including:

Electronic Music Studio, supporting classes in electronic and computer music, composition, recording, and music for moving image. Industry-standard hardware and software are refreshed each year. Support equipment includes a fully stocked electronics workbench for projects ranging from circuit building/bending to interactive instrument construction;

Music Technology Classroom, supporting a range of classes from electronic and computer music, to notation, recording, conducting, music education, and composition;

Virtual Rehearsal Room (VROOM), where students practice and rehearse in front of a "virtual audience" (via video) that simulates the movement, sounds, and interruptions that may be found at a live concert. The VROOM allows the student to choose from nine different virtual acoustical spaces and includes recording capability.

Eleanore Vail, pianist, arrived at Western College in 1947, having studied at the Eastman School of Music as a student colleague with three musicians who joined the Miami music faculty at about the same time that Eleanore came to Western College. Those musicians were Nicholas Poccia, George Seltzer, and Adon Foster. Eleanore Vail became Chair of the Music Department of Western College. She and Richard Monaco, composer, were dedicated music faculty of the Western College for many years. An interview with Eleanore in June, 2013, records her memories at Western:

> The Chair of the Music Department at Western, Harold Schmidt, hired me to teach piano. Long before I arrived, the well-known composer Edgar Stillman Kelley was in residence there. The cottage next to Presser Hall was built for him and his wife.
>
> Another member of the music faculty at the time was Ruth Bracher. Ruth was a very capable musician, having studied at the Cincinnati Conservatory and Yale University. When Ruth retired, they needed a replacement, and Richard Monaco came to fill the position. He had done graduate work at Cornell University where he received his PhD.
>
> Richard took over the choir and kept very current with repertoire for it. He also later established the Oxford Chamber Orchestra with Elizabeth Walker Lane as concertmistress. Other Miami music faculty played in the orchestra, including Everett Nelson and Nicholas Poccia. Some members of the orchestra came from Cincinnati. The cellist, Salvatore Silipigni, came from Ball State University to play. The orchestra lasted for about five years before the funding ran out. Programs that were performed included Mozart's *Concerto for Two Pianos K365* [Eleanore Vail and David Bean, pianists] and *Knoxville, Summer 1915*, by Samuel Barber.

Eleanor Vail concluded her 2013 interview as follows:

> I had some good students at Western, one of whom was Ann Rittle Monaco, who later had a private studio and became Assistant Director of the Merit School of Music for young students in Chicago. Another memorable student was Virginia Weckstrom Kantor, who had a distinguished career at the Cleveland Institute of Music and at the University of Texas, Houston, where she is a teacher and coach/accompanist. My career at Western was very enjoyable. Donna Shalala, although she was not a music student, was probably the most well-known graduate of Western College. She was in President Clinton's administration.

THE OXFORD CHORAL ENSEMBLE

The 1980s saw a growing interest in creating a community choral group open to singers dedicated to performing choral music of the classical repertoire. A document housed in the Smith Library of Regional History in Oxford describes the inception of the Oxford Choral Ensemble. "The core of the Ensemble was a group of young Oxford residents who wanted the opportunity to sing more varied repertoire than the local church choirs provided."

In 1982, a member of the Miami University music faculty, Dr. William Bausano, became the music director for the group. Dr. Frank Jordan, organist at Holy Trinity Episcopal Church in Oxford, became the accompanist. In December of that year, the Ensemble performed Part I of Handel's *Messiah* in Hall Auditorium on the campus of Miami University.

The Ensemble then established an annual schedule of two concerts per year, one in the spring and one in the fall. The December 1983 concert took the form of a madrigal dinner, the first of several in the years to come. The Smith Archives document provides information on the growth of the Ensemble:

> Singers new to Oxford were eager to join the ensemble, at times necessitating auditions. The concerts were well supported by the Oxford community, both in attendance and in donations used for expenses such as purchasing music.

In addition to standard works of older composers, the Ensemble also performed works of modern composers. One such composition was a setting of an Emily Dickinson poem by the distinguished choral composer James Mulholland. In March of 2003, the Ensemble performed Morten Lauridsen's new work *Lux Aeterna* with the composer present at a rehearsal. In December 2005, the Oxford Choral Ensemble gave its final concert.

Chapter Seventeen

Conclusion and Future

Year of the Arts

James Lentini began his tenure as Dean of the School of Fine Arts at Miami University in 2007. Prior to that he was the founding Dean of the School of Art, Media and Music at the College of New Jersey from 2003-2007. In 2013 he left Miami to accept the position of senior vice president for academic affairs and provost at Oakland University in Rochester, Michigan. During his tenure at Miami, the name of the School was changed to the School of Creative Arts. President David Hodge commented on Lentini's service at Miami, referring to Miami's newly-named School of Creative Arts: "Jim raised the expectations and success of the School of Creative Arts. He was the one who had the vision for the Year of the Arts, a vision that he pursued vigorously and to great effect."

Lentini, a composer and classical guitarist, received degrees in music from Wayne State University, Michigan State University and the University of Southern California. He has recorded numerous original compositions on the American Classics series of the Naxos label. He received the Andrés Segovia International Composition Award in 2002 for his work entitled *Westward Voyage*. His leadership during Miami University's 'Year of the Arts' in 2012 is discussed in the Conclusion of this book.

Toward the end of Dean Lentini's leadership, the School of Fine Arts, established in 1929, was re-named the School of Creative Arts. This new designation coincided with Miami University's designation of the year 2012 as the 'Year of the Arts' at Miami. Among special events celebrating this designation were a lecture by Wynton Marsalis, Director of the Lincoln Center Jazz Orchestra in New York City, and a gala performance at New

York's Carnegie Hall on October 7, 2012, featuring student and faculty musicians.

An article in the *Cincinnati Enquirer* made the announcement about the 'Year of the Arts' initiative.

> Miami University's president David C. Hodge has declared this season the "Year of the Arts." Unique concerts, art exhibitions and signature events are celebrating the strong history and the diverse array of arts on the Oxford campus. When the nation is economically and educationally challenged, it is a great time to make a statement about the arts, said James Lentini, Dean of the School of Fine Arts. "The arts are an integral part of everything we do. It's not just some extra item that students need to take," said Lentini, who is a guitarist and composer. "For me, it's a statement that we're committed to this . . ."

This Carnegie Hall celebration was a landmark in the history of the Department of Music, a symbol of many decades of achievement. As we move on through the twenty-first century, the University will need to consider the reputation of its Department of Music and to find ways of maintaining the high quality that has been achieved. A fine music school, both in terms of faculty and physical facilities, is expensive to maintain. However, it is no more expensive than maintaining a sports program, a strong science curricu-

Miami musicians performing at Carnegie Hall, New York, October 7, 2012. Photo by Jeff Sabo, Miami University.

lum, or any other worthwhile educational offering. The end result of dedicated support is richly rewarding to students and to society-at-large, and it contributes to the advancement of music in America. A popular saying in the early part of the twenty-first century is: A great nation deserves great art.

Elizabeth Reitz Mullenix joined the Miami faculty in 2006 as Chair and Professor of Theatre and artistic director/producer of Miami University Theatre. She assumed the role of interim dean in 2013, and was appointed Dean in 2014. Prior to joining Miami, Mullenix served at Illinois State University as an associate professor of theatre and in leadership roles including associate chair of theatre; director of graduate studies for the Department of Theatre; and associate dean of the College of Fine Arts. Mullenix received a bachelor's degree in theatre and in English from the University of Vermont; a master's in theatre studies from the University of Illinois, Champaign-Urbana; and a doctorate in theatre studies from the University of Illinois. A theatre historian, Mullenix writes about antebellum culture/theatre, cross-dressing, the American Civil War, first wave feminism and gender/feminist theory. In addition to many peer-reviewed journal articles and book chapters, she is author of *Wearing the Breeches: Gender on the Antebellum Stage* (2000). Her second monograph, *Theatres of War: Civil War Theatre and the Performance of Nationhood* is in progress.

CONCLUSION

The Department of Music at Miami University has been a part of Ohio's history for well over a century. Its impact as an educational resource for all Ohioans, as well as its service to out-of-state and out-of-country students is difficult to assess. But, if the on-campus quality of education enjoyed by Miami students is any indication, one would have to say that when the students graduate and leave the campus, they take with them an invaluable personal experience that is transferred into their own professional lives.

Over the years, one very positive aspect of this Department of Music was its sense of family sharing a common purpose amid losses as well as gains. The struggle and failure to preserve the Oxford String Quartet was one example of loss to the Department. Another example was the loss of the outstanding relationship with musicians in Luxembourg that was established under the leadership of John Heard as Chair of the Department. The educational value of such an international relationship for Miami's faculty and students seems to have been underestimated by those who made the decision to abandon this relationship.

The String Quartet functioned for decades as a proud symbol of the University's leadership in music, as well as a magnet for drawing artistically minded students and faculty to the University. The demise of the Department's connection with the Luxembourg Conservatory of Music and with the international Echternach Music Festival seems to have been parallel to the demise of the 'Miami Family' as it had been known through the course of the twentieth century. The opportunity to create an 'extended musical family' in Europe was lost.

Janelle Gelfand, the music critic for the Cincinnati Enquirer newspaper, published an article in 2007 that described one observer's estimation of what was happening to the music environment at Miami University. The article was entitled: "Sour notes at Miami University?"

> "Faculty Ensembles" still have a web page on the Miami University Music Department Web site. But word is, the university administration has now dissolved its Miami Wind Quintet, along with the distinguished Oxford String Quartet -- struggling along as a trio -- as the Enquirer announced last year. Further, pianist Ron J. Matson, who has been a fixture at Miami for 30 years, is nowhere to be found.
>
> And here's another worrisome note: Echternach (Luxembourg) International Festival Orchestra Miami project-which was successful for 15 years and the ONLY United States University/European professional festival orchestra connection of its kind in the U.S. -- has been discontinued.
>
> Exactly a year ago last January, I wrote that The Oxford Quartet was one of just two American quartets to celebrate its 60th birthday in 2006. The other was the Juilliard String Quartet. The region's only remaining all-faculty quartet is at Northern Kentucky University: The Azmari Quartet.
>
> It's obviously part of cost-cutting measures. A group of distraught fans in Oxford, Cincinnati and as far away as Cologne, Germany, campaigned last year to "save the quartet." They said the school's prestige was at stake. But the dean of MU's School of Fine Arts, Jose Antonio Bowen, stood firm.
>
> Bowen has moved on to a new post. But I can't help but think, especially as I sat at Henry Meyer's memorial last night, that an era has ended.
>
> Where are the resident ensembles in local universities? Are they dinosaurs?

One must speak of the tremendous progress of the Department of Music during its first century of existence. One of the most significant accomplishments was the building of the Center for Performing Arts that opened in 1969, minus the large auditorium originally in the plans. This building brought under one roof a Department that had seen inferior physical facilities for decades. Another accomplishment was the increased quality of students and the variety of course offerings. Leaders with vision will no doubt bring further accomplishments in the future.

When the Western College for Women closed in 1974, after one hundred twenty-one years of operation, Miami University purchased the campus and established what was known as the Miami University Western College program, offering students a Bachelor of Philosophy degree. This program lasted for several years and was finally abandoned in the 1990s. At one point in the existence of this program, the faculty involved in the program nourished a concept that they called 'ways of knowing,' which explained that knowledge is gained through channels other than book learning, such as intuition and aesthetic perception. It must be pointed out that intuition and aesthetic perception are some of the important lessons taught in the study of music that often are not accessed in other disciplines.

This particular Department of Music stands as a good example of what such departments all over the United States have to contend with in terms of the political and financial fluctuations from one period to another. Public institutions are especially impacted by these fluctuations. Furthermore, academic institutions evolve differently depending upon the attitudes of their governing bodies. The particular physical facility needs of programs may go unnoticed because of other program priorities that take precedence.

The reader will have learned from this historical account that Miami University has attained over the decades a present position as a leader among public universities. However, also documented in this history is an example of how music at a university can sometimes be relegated to a lesser position among other priorities that a given administration might have. Therefore, full support of music and the arts will often be found wanting in comparison with support given to other areas. Thus, the political climate at any given moment in history may or may not be favorable to the growth of music and the arts. A prime example is the fact that a basic physical facility, an auditorium originally intended to be built adjacent to the Center for Performing Arts strictly for musical performance, never materialized.

Leonardo da Vinci is quoted as saying, "The soul is composed of harmony." Those words, spoken centuries ago, should be taken more seriously in today's society, given the level of discord that we see today in our midst. We need a great deal of leadership on this subject from inspired individuals who will dare to face the odds created by a system that fails to comprehend fully the significance of Leonardo's thought. The category of music that society calls 'art music' possesses the unique ability to probe deeply into the human soul for those who accept it into their lives. The concept of 'soul' has been eroded to a point at which it seems to be a rather foreign concept in present-day society. But, musicians of today are keenly aware that the soul does exist and that it needs the proper nourishment. Thus, music faculties everywhere continue to share this knowledge with the next generations of students.

It is worth repeating a statement by the Florida Music Educators Association that was mentioned earlier in the book:

> Music and the Fine Arts have been a significant portion of every culture's educational system for more than 3,000 years. The human brain has been shown to be "hard-wired" for music; there is a biological basis for music being

> an important part of human experience. Music and the Arts surround daily life in our present day culture. Most present day artists, architects, and musicians acquired their interests during public school Fine Arts classes . . . Education without the Fine Arts is fundamentally impoverished and subsequently leads to an impoverished society.

One must conclude that the survival of the arts over the centuries is due to their innate power to supply human need, and not necessarily due to the vicissitudes of political decisions favoring or disfavoring their inclusion in educational institutions. Thus, a group of politicians may proclaim the need to cut funding for the arts; but those decisions, though frustrating to artists, are always only temporary and incapable of any serious repression of the artistic impulse. If society were able to perceive this fact, there could be great strides made toward a healthier nation.

In our time, there has been much research on the advantages of music to individuals and society at large. Nevertheless, it would seem that many of our politicians and educational leaders do not read the results of such research, given the fact that budgets for music and the arts are routinely cut in times of financial stress.

It has been the intent of the author that the history documented in this book be not only a tribute to the Miami music professors and the students who passed through the halls of the Department of Music at Miami, but also that this Department should be seen as a cross-section of the country's music schools that continue to work toward building a better society, knowing that music aids in that task. The reader will have noticed how often graduates of the Department have commented about the major influence on them of their music professors. Thus we see the continuity of the art moving into the future by way of the apprenticeship model.

The reader will also have noticed the impressive array of internationally renowned musicians with whom the Miami faculty studied, thus bringing to Miami University a wealth of background and expertise, and the educational aspect of the original Artists Series at Miami that introduced students to numerous internationally renowned artists bringing a depth of musical knowledge to enrich the Miami experience.

During the 1960s and 70s, Miami's Department of Music experienced the positive impact of the nation's strong economical growth. But later, as the twentieth century closed and we moved into the next century, economic factors put some restraints on higher education in general. Of course, the popularity and student demand for any program is a key factor in the program's success. Fortunately, at Miami University the student demand for the music offerings remained strong into the second decade of the twenty-first century.

However, tuition costs for students continued to rise, causing financial stress on families that far exceeded the financial demands of earlier decades. A sad commentary on today's institutions of higher learning is that the nation's college students are being burdened with the unprecedented cost of education, so that they are forced to take out student loans resulting in debts that must be paid off as they enter the work force. Surely, this is an unfair burden that demands national attention and political change. In spite of this, the passion for music continues among the young generations, and this will continue to keep alive the music programs at universities.

SELF-STUDY AND THE MISSION

During the 1970s and beyond, the Department of Music (as well as other departments at Miami University) underwent several self-studies, during the course of which the faculty was involved in retreats for intensive discussion of its mission. It was also a time when the University was exploring a growing need for outreach and service beyond the bounds of the campus, a view of a university's role in society that was beginning to emerge in American institutions. One might say that the same kind of self-study imposed upon departments of a university could also be applied to the administration. It might prove quite valuable for members of the upper administration to hold retreats at which careful analysis of priorities are discussed. Administrators will be quick to say that this is already being done. At any rate, future success of higher education in music and the arts will always depend on careful analysis of the facility needs as well as faculty needs for these programs. In this modern age of private donors, this message must be sent to them.

The Department's activities through the decades were prime examples of outreach and service. Audiences throughout Ohio and beyond were given the gift of music through the performances of such faculty groups as the Oxford String Quartet and the Miami Wind Quintet, as well as countless student ensemble performances of the Miami University Glee Club, Choraliers, Collegiate Chorale, Wind Ensemble, Symphony Band, Orchestra, and many faculty and student soloists.

The mission of providing outreach and service to humanity is ultimately the goal of the arts. Added to that, of course, is the immeasurable value that music provides for the individual spiritual and aesthetic life of our youth. If we as a nation want to advance beyond the materialistic view of life to a more balanced society, then the arts will have to be taken more seriously. Both public and private schools all over the nation must choose leaders who are aware of this philosophical understanding of the arts.

However, it is not only political and academic leaders who must come to grips with the value of music. University students themselves must undergo a fundamental change in their attitude toward campus performances. Those events are too often viewed as merely a source of casual entertainment instead of something of real educational value. While it is true that music does provide entertainment and a healthy alternative to the mundane daily routine, there is the deeper aspect of discovery and self-realization that is available to all who approach music with that frame of mind. What seems little understood is that music is truly a language for the purpose of communicating ideas. Only as we grasp the full import of this concept shall we become enlightened and fully educated.

In the old days of Miami University when enrollment was small, the entire student body used to gather in the auditorium each morning for convocation. These community gatherings had the advantage of bonding the student body and giving importance to the various campus offerings of free lectures and concerts. This concept was tried within the Department of Music when Dr. Paul Aliapoulios was Chair. Periodic convocations of the music students were held in the recital hall for general dissemination of thoughts from the faculty.

The performance organizations of the Department of Music present a multitude of campus performances each year for the benefit of all. The student body of the University has access to all of these wonderful performances that allow one personal growth through discovery, intuition and inspiration.

THE DEPARTMENT QUESTIONING ITS ROLE

During the 1980s, many faculty discussions within the Department of Music were concerned with the perception of the Department's role held by the University community as well as by the State of Ohio. It would seem that, as time moved on there was a tendency for miscommunication between the 'workers' and the 'employers,' as it were. Leaders at the University's top level and at the State level were developing their own concept of how a music program should fit into the overall academic resources.

Some claim that politics and art do not mix. Others who are more pragmatic claim that politics is always in charge, no matter how altruistic one's view may be. Perhaps a better way to express the relationship between politics and art is to say that, by their very nature the two are not a match made in heaven, but that coexistence is inevitable.

Regardless of the reasons behind the political decisions that were made at the University and State levels, the ultimate effect was to cause the Department to question its role as an educational entity. Some would say that society has always been fickle with respect to its views of the arts and the role that they play in our lives. There are always forces that go against the freedom and survival of the arts. But, apparently there is a power in the arts that protects them from eclipse. One has only to recall how the Parisians worked feverishly to remove the precious art works from the Louvre and hide them from the Nazis during the War, or how the Jewish inmates at the concentration camps formed musical groups to keep music in their lives during their incarceration.

In institutions where enormous financial resources are available from private donors to support sports and other areas of interest to the donors, music may often take a back seat, unless similar donors are found to support it. This is unfortunate in that it can create an imbalance between the humanities and other areas of the academy.

FUTURE MUSIC STUDENTS

In the fall of 2012 the enrollment in the Department of Music included twenty-six graduate students, one hundred and five Bachelor of Music students and forty-four Bachelor of Arts students. Academically speaking, modern educational requirements at liberal arts institutions, such as Miami University, have placed a rather large burden upon music students. Their academic load of course work, in addition to the great demands of mastering their vocal and instrumental specialties, is often a source of frustration for them. And yet, if they are able to achieve the necessary discipline and hard work, this fashions them into exceptionally strong leaders in the areas of performance and music education.

From a student perspective, the college years comprise an unforgettable period in one's life. The human bonds and friendships with both faculty members and other students belong to a time of life unlike any other, a time that enriches one beyond measure. The Department of Music at Miami University over the decades has been a place in which the one-on-one faculty/student learning environment has proven itself to be of unique value in an age of increasing impersonal relationships. This kind of mentoring, akin to the old apprenticeship system, is irreplaceable. The human element in passing a musical education from master to student cannot be tossed out in favor of some antiseptic technological approach.

In the twenty-first century, there is a tendency for university administrators everywhere to forget the importance of maintaining faculty stability in order to recruit quality students wanting to study with teachers of established reputations. In an age of financial exigencies, it is easy to make the mistake of replacing established tenured faculty with visiting appointments in order to save money. But, in the end this may have the effect of turning away students looking for an institution where stability reigns and proves itself in providing quality education.

The Department of Music is more than just a workplace for its faculty and more than just a classroom or studio for its students. It is a place where both faculty and students gather to speak the ancient and beloved language of music that is common to all generations.

Much is being discussed these days about an approach to educating students that will inspire them and result in responsible and productive citizens. One theory espoused by many is that there must be a focus upon the individual student. In the apprenticeship system used for training musicians, we find this ideal in action. The one-on-one relationship of student and teacher can do much to create the student's self-image and increase confidence. The public performance requirement for students of music adds to this positive educational environment.

Many readers of this book will realize the value of music in our public schools. Those of us who have witnessed the joy in our young people from participation in school choirs, bands and orchestras know how much music adds to the growth and maturity of the young. Talented instructors are dedicated to providing quality musical experiences for their students. There are graduates of the Miami University Department of Music who are devoting careers to the musical education of the next generations.

MUSIC AT MIAMI: THE FUTURE

In spite of the evidence that music has the power to create a bonding among members of society, the future of music at Miami University may not be bright. At least one member of the music faculty at Miami in 2013 was of the opinion that by the year 2033 the University could quite possibly have no Department of Music at all. Given the national political climate of the country in 2013, this prediction did not seem overly pessimistic.

However, as in the case of a doctor's prognosis of terminal illness, it is always wise to get a second opinion. If the successes of Miami's music faculty and alumni are any indication, one would think that the Department of Music can look forward to its ability to attract generations of music students to come.

It can be argued that higher education originally focused upon the pursuit of goodness, beauty and truth, with less concern for the pursuit of a degree to function as a work permit in society. The statement of the Florida Music Educators Association, presented in the Introduction of this book, speaks to that proposition, as does the statement by Dr. Shilo Shaffer Myers that was reported in the May, 1906 edition of *The Miami Recensio* and included in Chapter Two above. It would seem that a materialistic way of life has eroded much of those primary values. Perhaps the future of the arts will, to a degree, depend upon a general change of course from materialism to the more spiritual values.

It is necessary to explain a fact regarding any music faculty that can be easily overlooked, a fact that has an impact on any musical academy. The fact is that performing musicians who make up a music faculty maintain their freshness as music experts by performing in faculty ensembles such as a string quartet, a woodwind quintet, a brass quintet, etc. This activity strengthens the teaching quality in faculty studios as well as serving as a recruitment tool. High School students shopping for a college to attend will be attracted to a school that showcases its faculty in public performance. Professor Andrea Ridilla sums it up this way: "My performances with the Miami Wind Quintet were an excellent recruiting tool. Faculty ensembles such as the Wind Quintet, and the Oxford String Quartet inspired students to choose Miami for their training because these faculty groups serve as professional models of performance excellence."

It is not generally understood that, for performing musicians, faculty performance is the equivalent of scholarly research. In other disciplines of academia, faculty members use the writings of world scholars to strengthen and augment their work in the classroom and for sending their findings into the general public arena. For performing musicians, the published works of composers must be studied in great detail for presentation to the public. Therefore, to deprive a music faculty of the historically established research outlets for their art, such as a string quartet or some other chamber group, is to diminish the overall effectiveness of their reason for serving as teachers and mentors to the student body.

In the twenty-first century, universities all over America are experiencing great change, largely due to technology. More and more online courses are being offered in which professor and student are separated from one another into physically remote spaces. In the case of music instruction, this method may lack the acoustically desirable atmosphere that surrounds both mentor and apprentice in the conventional studio setting. Live musical creativity depends upon the mutual acoustic experience within the common space of a studio in order for maximum understanding of the subject matter.

Traditionally, higher education has relied upon students gathering together at a physical campus where they are given the opportunity to mix with young people of all different backgrounds and aspirations. The language of music requires this kind of human experience in order to bond its participants. Indeed, in its large definition music must rely upon the shared experience of many, in the same manner as a community of scholars and students relies upon a common spoken language for their communication.

Miami University has evolved from its small humble beginnings in the early nineteenth century into a major public institution with a well-planned campus to enhance the interactions of its students and faculty. It has been a place for students to explore and to 'speak' the ancient language of music so that the art form may continue its major contribution to society. It now stands at a crossroads in society's transition from the traditional to the experimental. One must hope that its leaders will be inspired to realize its potential for providing a model of excellence as a residential student community amid the temptations to abandon this system of training future generations.

In 1979, Ernest L. Boyer, President of the Carnegie Foundation for the Advancement of Teaching, was guest speaker at the fiftieth anniversary of the School of Fine Arts at Miami University. At the close of his remarks, delivered at the Miami University Art Museum, he left his audience with the following words.

> In November, 1920, at the annual meeting of The National Association of State Universities in Washington, President R. M. Hughes of Miami University was assigned the indefinite topic: "The Most Important University Problem." President Hughes in response to that open ended question declared that: "It may not be the most urgent problem from the University standpoint, but tremendously urgent from the point of view of the country." He proposed that the university become the patron of creative artists and bring great art to campuses. The press response was enthusiastic. Walter Lippman called it "a most enlightened business." *Colliers* called it "A New Hope for Artists," and *The Christian Science Monitor* said that, "For a bold step forward of the progressive ideal…Keep an eye on the little town of Oxford, Ohio."

A nation that loses is Muse loses its Soul

Appendix A

Music Faculty as of October 2010

Albin (1975), BM Indian University, MM Wichita State University, Doctor of Education, Indiana University

Averbach (2002) BM State Music Academy (Bulgaria), MM Bulgarian National Academy of Music, PhD University of Michigan

Bausano (1981) BM Ed Northern Michigan University, MM & DMA University of Southern California

Boge (1986) BM U. of Dayton, MM & PhD University of Michigan

Davis (1990) BM Berklee College of Music, MM & Doctoral degree Ohio State University

Delzell (1999) BM University of Wisconsin-Madison, MM Concordia College, PhD Concordia College

Edwards (2001) BM Ohio University, MM & PhD Arizona State University University

Garcia (2005) BM The Juilliard School, MM Juilliard, MM Juilliard, MM University of Massachusetts, PhD, Duke University

Gingras (1986) BM Montreal Music Conservatory, Canada, MM Northwestern

Green (2005) PhD University of Illinois, Advanced Studies *Technische Universität,* Berlin, Germany

Harris (1988) BM Ind. U., MM University of Wisconsin-Milwaukee, MFA

Kernodle (1997) BM Virginia State University, MA Ohio State University, DMA University of Southern California

Mitchell (1988) BM Arizona State University, MM Ariz. St., DMA Arizona State University

Morales-Matos (1997) BM Indiana University, MM University of Cincinnati College-Conservatory of Music
Olcott (1978) B.A. San Francisco State University, MM Manhattan School of Music
Opatz-Muni (1997) BM Ed U. of Northern Iowa, MM University of Northern Iowa
Phillips (1990) BM Eastman School of Music, MM Bowling Green State University
Ridilla (1987) BM Oberlin College; MM The Juilliard School of Music
Smolder (2002) BA Anderson Broaddus College, MM University of Kentucky
Speck (1988) BM Baylor University, MM University of Michigan
Siok Tan (1999) BM, MM, & PhD University of Cincinnati College-Conservatory of Music
Tanner (1996) BM West Virginia University, MM Miami, PhD West Virginia University
Thomas (1982) BM West Virginia University, MM Indiana University, PhD Indiana University
Thurmer (1997) BM University of Tennessee, MM New England Conservatory, MA Colorado Christian University, PhD University of Miami

PART-TIME

Heather MacPhail, Staff Accompanist
Allison Acord, voice
Audrey Luna, voice
Jim McCutcheon, guitar (1979)
Stephen Ullery, bass
Jacquelyn Davis, harp

NEW FACULTY AFTER 2010

Rebecca Andres, flute
David M. Bell, Music Education
Elizabeth Hoover musicology
Amy Kiradjieff, violin
Tze Jean Lim, violin
Frank Huang, piano
Douglas Lindsay, trumpet
Jeremy Long, jazz ensembles
Morrigan O'Brien Kane, flute
Steven Pride, trumpet

Linda McAlister, voice
Carson McTeer, tuba
Jeremy Jones, conductor/choral music
Per Boland, composition/technology
Michael LaMattina, percussion
Stephen Lytle, symphonic band/marching band
Christin Schillinger, bassoon
Bruce Murray, piano, Department Chair

Appendix B

Non-tenured & Temporary Faculty; Part-time & Adjunct Faculty; and Branch Campus Faculty

This list includes faculty from different decades. Unfortunately, although biographies for these faculty members are available, space in this volume does not permit their inclusion.

NON-TENURED & TEMPORARY FACULTY

Frederick Gersten, voice; Michael Andres, saxophone; Eddye Pierce Berry, voice
William Brice, flute; Erich Lear, violin; Karen Andrie, cello
Carmon DeLeone, condictor; Haden McKay, cello; Steven Craig, oboe
Paul Metz, theory; Linda Trotter-Heger, voice; George Tepping, voice
Alma Jean Smith, voice; Susan Walker, violin; Mary Stanton, piano

PART-TIME & VISITING FACULTY

Lee Suman, music education
Mary Jane Cope, piano
Edwin Domb, organ
Jeffrey Williams, trombone
Sandra Williams, music education
Jean Schneider, piano
Brad Caldwell, accompanist
David van Abbema, voice

Victor Polonsky, piano
Hal Grossman, violin
James McCutcheon, guitar
John Bercaw, jazz history
Michael Chertock, piano
Jeffrey Multer, violin
Eric Pritchard, violin

ADJUNCT FACULTY

For many years, professional musicians from the Cincinnati Symphony Orchestra and the Dayton Philharmonic Orchestra were employed in Miami's Department of Music as adjunct professors teaching the various orchestral instruments. Gradually, during the 1970s and 1980s, the Department was able to secure funding for tenured positions in the various instrumental studios. The musicians listed below held positions as adjunct teachers prior to the shift to tenured faculty positions:

Ferde Priore, oboe, Cincinnati Symphony
Roger Miller, oboe, Dayton Philharmonic
Marie Speziale, trumpet, Cincinnati Symphony
Richard Topper, string bass, Cincinnati Symphony
Jack Wellbaum, flute, Cincinnati Symphony
Martin James, bassoon, Cincinnati Symphony
Michael Andres, saxophone
W. Edwin Domb, organ
Eleanor Vail, collaborative pianist
Harold Byers, violin, Cincinnati Symphony
Tony Chipburn, trombone, Cincinnati Symphony
Otto Eifert, bassoon, Cincinnati Symphony
Stanley P. George, trombone
John Reger, trombone, Dayton Philharmonic
Gary Johnson, trombone

BRANCH CAMPUS FACULTY

Middletown Campus

Jack Armstrong, percussion, associate 1972–73
David E. Jones, strings, associate 1972–74
William F. Stiehl, band, associate 1972–77
Mariann Clinton, part-time instructor 1972–77
Lola Markworth, woodwinds, associate 1972–78

Helen Ramsdell, voice, associate 1972–80
J. Earl Jones, brass, associate 1972–81
Ann Monaco, voice, lecturer 1973–75
Janet Houser, lecturer 1973–77
Christine Parker, full-time instructor 1973–1996
Joan Gersten, voice, lecturer 1974–75
Cheryl Saunders, lecturer 1974–75
Helen Blair Smith 1977–79
Mary Lautensleger, 1980–81
Susan Joyce, instructor 1996–2015
James McCutcheon, guitar, instructor 1996-continuing

Hamilton Campus

Bois Elwell, part-time choral director 1972–74
Mariann Clinton, part-time instructor 1972–76
Samuel D. Shie 1975–77

Part-time/Visiting Faculty, Unavailable Information

Raymond Brandhof, saxophonist 1972–75
P. L. Stone 1970s

Appendix C

Miami Opera Productions 1998–2012

DIRECTOR OF OPERA, MARI OPATZ-MUNI

1998–1999: The Old Maid and the Thief (Menoti), and Riders to the Sea (Vaughan Williams); José-Luis Novo, Conductor; James Haffner, Stage Director

1999–2000: Albert Herring (Britten); José-Luis Novo, Conductor; Tim Ocel, Stage Director

2000–2001: Trouble in Tahiti (Bernstein), and Gianni Schicchi (Puccini); Bradley Thachuk, Conductor; Jay Jackson, Stage Director

2001–2002: Hansel and Gretel (Humperdinck); Bradley Thachuk, Conductor; Brian Robertson, Stage Director

2002–2203: Pirates of Penzance (Gilber & Sullivan); Ricardo Averbach, Conductor; Brian Robertson, Stage Director

2003–2004: La Perichole

2004–2005: Le Nozze di Figaro (Mozart); Ricardo Averbach, Conductor; Sally Stunkel, Stage Director

2005–2006: Cosi fan Tutte (Mozart); Ricardo Averbach, Conductor; Gary Briggle, Stage Director

2006–2007 Die Fledermaus (Strauss); Ricardo Averbach, Conductor; Buz Davis, Stage Director

2007–2008: The Magic Flute (Mozart); Ricardo Averbach, Conductor: Mihaela Bogdan, Stage Director

2008–2009: Paul Bunyan (Britten); Benjamin Smolder, Conductor; Erik Friedman, Stage Director

2009–2010: Suor Angelica (Puccini) & Gianni Schicchi (Puccini); Ricardo Averbach and Benjamin Smolder, Conductors; Mihaela Bogdan, Stage Diretcor

2010–2011: Cendrillon (Massenet); Ricardo Averbach, Conductor; Nicholas Muni, Stage Director

2011–2012: The Pirates of Penance (Gilbert & Sullivan); Ricardo Averbach, Conductor; Jack Liles, Assoc. Conductor, Nicholas Wuehrmann, Stage Director

2012–2013: Trial By Jury (Gilbert & Sullivan), The Face on the Barroom Floor (Henry Mollicone), and Trouble in Tahiti (Bernstein); Ricardo Averbach and Jack Liles, Conductors; Nicholas Muni, Stage Director

2012–2014: Averbach and Jack Liels, Conductors; Nicholas Muni, Stage Director

Appendix D

Miami University Musicals 1980–2007

JACK LILES: MUSICAL DIRECTOR/CONDUCTOR

The Music Man '80,
Brigadoon '81
Hello Dolly '81
West Side Story '82
Annie Get your Gun '82
The Fantastics '82
Chicago '83
Damn Yankees '83
Company '84
Grease '84
Oklahoma '85
Joseph and the Dreamcoat '85,'02
A Chorus Line '86
Anything Goes '86
1940's Radio Hour '86
Shenandoah '87
Kiss Me Kate '87
Annie '88
Is There Life After High School '87
Pirates of Penzance '88
The Pajama Game '89
The Mystery of Edwin Drood '90
Into the Woods '91

Big River '91
Man of La Mancha '92
Gypsy '92
Assassins '93
Sweet Charity '93
Oh What a Lovely War '94
Cabaret '95
Sunday in the Park With George '95
The Secret Garden '96
She Loves Me '97
Merrily We Roll Along '97
Falsettoland '98
Oliver '99
Lady in the Dark '00
On this Island '01
State Fair '01
Green Gables '03
Boys from Syracuse '03
Hair '05
Seussical '07
Opera: Pirates of Penzance '11 (Associate Conductor)
Trouble in Tahiti '12 (Musical Director/Conductor)

Appendix E

Interviews with Faculty and Graduates

In 2013, the author interviewed faculty and graduates to gather their thoughts about Miami University and their memories of faculty and fellow students. Their stories often reveal a quality of life within the Department of Music that speaks to the enjoyment of their student days.

One story comes from Professor Gary Holt of the *Hochschule fur Musik* in Cologne, Germany, who received his undergraduate and Master's degrees in cello from Miami during the early 1970s when Otto Frohlich was Conductor of the Miami University Symphony Orchestra. Professor Holt relates the following episodes.

We really tried to irritate our conductor of the Miami Symphony Orchestra, Otto Frohlich, as much as possible without being too rude. I must confess, that I was basically the initiator of all this business.

One of our first endeavors was to form an "Oxford Violoncello Society". We had big sunflower yellow badges made, which we proudly wore on our suits and dresses during concerts. The audience could not help but noticing them. Our next idea was to buy bright colored socks for the men, preferably a different color for each leg. Naturally we had to roll our pants legs up a bit to expose the socks. Another time we put a "Playboy" pin-up photo in his score. When he came upon it, his glance naturally went immediately to the 'cello section. One joke we decided to do only during rehearsal. We were rehearsing Tchaikovsky's 1812 Overture which begins in the violas and 'cellos with an introduction similar to a Russian hymn. Only six players perform it. So the six of us transposed it into a different key. You can imagine the look on his face when the woodwinds came in later and our harmony clashed rudely with what they were playing.

INTERVIEW WITH DAVID COPE, ON COMPOSER KAREL HUSA

I brought him [Karel Husa] as guest composer for a New Music Festival I ran at Miami University in Ohio, where he conducted many of his works including Apotheosis of This Earth, an extraordinary piece for wind ensemble and now rewritten for full orchestra. Again, the musical energy he brought to the musicians and audience was inspiring.

I am dumbfounded when I now see lists of well-known twentieth-century composers of great merit and not find his name there. While much of his early work, for better or worse, was composed for bands and wind ensembles and then later orchestrated, I can't imagine that critics should be so blinded as to suspect his work of lesser merit because of that. Maybe it was his stranger in a strange land accent and demeanor that make them leave his work behind. But such things did not prevent Varèse or Stravinsky from finding places there.

Maybe one day, I hope while he still lives, his music and name will find a proper place in the lofty heights of important composers of recent vintage.

INTERVIEW WITH DAVID COPE, ON COMPOSER DONALD ERB

Sometime during the mid-1970s, I invited Don Erb to be guest composer for a new music festival I planned. I had known Don for many years and respected his music. I also had an ulterior motive for my invitation—the performance of one of his lesser-known works.

During the weeks prior to his visit, I did the necessary groundwork to prepare for the performance of this piece, which included visiting various shops in the Cincinnati area, as well as a few non-music departments on the Miami University campus in Ohio where I then taught.

As the dates of the festival approached, I swore everyone who knew about this special performance to secrecy. By the time the work's various paraphernalia was ready, no one but those bound by promise knew anything about what was soon going to happen to them.

Souvenir is not an ordinary work. It begins in complete darkness with a small orchestra surrounding the audience. Slowly the sound moves around the hall much as the 'wave' might at a baseball game. It gathers in intensity as dancers slowly appear on stage, clothed in special outfits that respond to black light projected on their bodies that then appear to glow in the dark.

As Souvenir continues, giant air-filled balloons spill onto the stage, they too sensitive to black light. The dancers bounce these balloons, ranging in size from beach balls to weather balloons—hence my early shopping for these props. The dancers then direct the balls toward the audience and, what theater people call the fourth wall breaks. In other words, the audience now becomes part of the show, bouncing the balls around whether they want to or not.

With the music becoming faster and yet louder, the performers point cans of Silly String, that black-light sensitive stuff that looks like it stains but doesn't, and spray the audience and balls still bouncing around the room. The melee begins.

Near the end of the performance, something very special occurs. Unknown to the anyone but the few who'd helped me, the ceiling has been filled with black-light sensitive Ping-Pong balls, made possible by a large net strung from the heights. Once released, the balls fall into the audience as, of course, souvenirs. By this time, covered with silly string, still bouncing balloons, and bombarded by Ping-Pong balls, whatever has passed for a performance has disappeared. Everybody simply has fun.

INTERVIEW WITH JOHN HEARD, ON STUDENT/FACULTY PROGRAMS

An international cooperative was created for students and faculty (1992–1998) when the Prague Conservatory of Music and the Prague Wind Quintet exchanged performances. A second cooperative existed from 1996–2005 with a series of performances involving Miami music faculty and graduate students with Venezuelan musicians from the Simon Bolivar Philharmonic Orchestra, National Symphony Orchestra of Venezuela, and the Simon Bolivar Conservatory of Music, in Caracas and Colonia Tovar, Venezuela.

The "Creative Student Enhancement Fund" was established, with donor Virginia Glick supporting the fund to aid student participation in the Echternach Festival Orchestra in Luxembourg and other student travel to juried competitions and performances in distinctive venues.

In 1989, a Graduate String Quartet was formed in cooperation with the Dean of Fine Arts by offering graduate assistantships.

From 1993–1996 I assisted the Miami voice faculty in developing cooperative initiatives between the Miami opera program and the Whitewater/Sorg Opera Companies in Middletown, Ohio, and Richmond, Indiana.

I established the Undergraduate Artists Competition in the Department and identified Mr. Geoffrey Hall as a donor to fund it. His gift was matched by a grant from the First Boston Corporation of Atlanta. With this help, plus the assistance of the University Development Office and Mr. Henry Jung, the Competition funding was insured.

With funding from Paul and Virginia Glick, weekly radio programs of student and faculty performances over WMUB-FM radio were broadcast from 1994–1997. The series was entitled "Miami Music Hall."

INTERVIEW WITH ANDREA RIDILLA, ON TEACHING AND PERFORMING

For the past 12 years, I have been performing in solo and orchestral music festivals in Europe each summer. In addition, I have been performing in South America and Russia. I often take one of my students to play 2nd oboe with me in the music festivals in which I perform. This experience proves to be a seminal experience in their careers. International connections are valuable for recruitment in the global market in which our current students will develop careers.

My performances with the faculty Wind Quintet were an excellent recruiting tool. Faculty ensembles such as the Wind Quintet and the Oxford String Quartet inspired students to choose Miami for their training because these faculty groups serve as professional models of performance excellence

My principal position at Miami is in oboe performance, and my research takes me abroad frequently. In April 2012, I was invited to give master classes at Moscow Tchaikovsky Conservatory of Music and the St. Petersburg Rimsky-Korsakov Conservatory. In 2012–13, I was invited by the U.S. Department of State to perform and teach in the Russian Far East in Vladivostok in October and March for two weeks each. I also performed last season at the Musica no Museu series in Rio de Janeiro, Brazil. In May 2013, I was invited by Lorée {Oboes} of Paris as one of five international solo oboists to perform at the Monteverdi Solo Oboe Festival in Bolzano-Bozen, Italy, where I was the only American artist.

My reed making research led me to develop an oboe gouging machine, which is currently sold on the global market. The machine is U.S. Patented. I am co-author, with Udo Heng, of the German firm, Reeds 'n Stuff, on a U.S. Patent for it and Miami University holds the patent.

In July 2012 I was co-host of the International Double Reed Society Conference held on the Miami University campus. This resulted in over 1,000 of international double reeds artists from 27 countries and 41 U.S. states performing and attending many concerts, lectures and master classes over five days.

Each Spring I teach an Honors course, "Discovering Italian Opera," a course, which I created in 2007 as a result of a grant to research opera in Italy for a summer. In this course, students have the opportunity to go on a field trip to the Metropolitan Opera in New York City. We travel by van, a wonderful bonding experience and stay for three nights, two nights of them in the

City. Students have the rare experience to attend a private pre-opera lecture at the Juilliard School presented by Fred Plotkin, Juilliard faculty member and author of the course text, "Opera 101." The trip is funded in-part by the Miami University Honors Program. Several of my students, mostly from the Farmer School of Business, have gone to careers in New York City and have joined the MET Young Associates, a program for early career opera aficionados. Requiring a $1,000 annual tax-deductible fee, members are invited to receptions before opera where they can network and get to know new people in the City. Miami graduates who took my course have joined this group and it has helped them to make new contacts in Manhattan while developing their passion for opera. In 2012, I was a recipient of the Miami University Associated Student Government (ASG) Outstanding Professor Award, nominated by a student in one of my opera courses.

Appendix F

Donors to the Building of the Center for Performing Arts

MUSIC LIBRARY, CENTER FOR PERFORMING ARTS

Named the "William T. and Dorothy R. Amos Music Library (1972). William Amos was a 1931 graduate of Miami University and was Secretary of the Sidney Printing & Publishing Company as well as Editor of the Sidney, Ohio, *Daily News.*

SIDNEY W. SOUERS RECITAL HALL, CENTER FOR PERFORMING ARTS

Rear Admiral Souers was appointed as the first Director of U.S. Central Intelligence on January 23, 1946 by President Harry Truman.
  1892 Born Dayton, Ohio
  1914 A.B., Miami University; member of the Kappa chapter of Delta Kappa Epsilon

Appendix G

Music Scholarships & Awards

Alice Mattmueller Alexander Memorial Voice Award
Alumni Music Award
George Barron Music Scholarship
Jeffrey J. Blank Scholarship
Nina J. Boyd Music Education Scholarship
Dr. Richard Cambridge Memorial Scholarship
Campus Owls Scholarship
Frances Cole Memorial Scholarship
Louise Glasgow and Eric E. Erickson Piano Scholarship
Cynthia Boeke Fisher Memorial Award
Pamela Fox Music History Award
Friends of Opera and Grand Night Award
Virginia Pierce Glick Music Education Scholarship
Darrell and Wilma Grothen Music Scholarship
The L. Eugene Hill Composition Prize
George R. and Galen Glasgow Hoxie Scholarship (alternates with art)
Jean Hartsock-Palmer Scholarship
Christopher B. Huff Memorial Award
Andrew Hummel Memorial Scholarship
Alberta Lutz Ittel Music Education Scholarship
Lacey/Strimple Highland Band and Drum Scholarship
Lois D. Lehmkuhl Owl Award
NFMC Herman and Mary Neuman Music Award
Ohio Music Teachers Association Scholarship
Piano Academic and Musical Achievement Award

Pam Eileen Poccia Award
Elizabeth Potteiger Cello Award
Presser Foundation Scholarship
Kapra Merideth Quain Memorial Scholarship
Nina Palmer Quay Memorial Scholarship
Mary Evans Rees Memorial Scholarship
Richard L. Schilling Music Education Scholarship
Dona Clare Sheley Presidential Scholarship
Steven Shumway String Scholarship
Richard A. Steuk Music Award
Clyde E. And Alice W. Stiner Scholarship
Jane Scott Hayes Telfair Music Education Scholarship
Tom & Carol Tierney Piano Award
Barbara J. Tuttle Memorial Scholarship
Walt & Marcia Wood Scholarship
W. C. Cummings Award
Deutsch Music Award
William E. Schmidt Foundation Vocal Music Scholarship
Virginia Dolohan Goebel-Fisher Music Education Scholarship
Everett Nelson Music Scholarship

Appendix H

List of Interviewees

David Cope, Resident Composer, 1973–1978
Nicolas Poccia, Emeritus
Steven Reineke, Alumnus
Dr. David Felder, Alumnus
Elizabeth Walker-Lane, Emerita
Gary Holt, Alumnus
Dr. Paul Aliapoulios, Chair, Dept. of Music, 1972–1976
Mari Opatz-Muni, Director of Opera, 1998–2012
Adon Foster, Emeritus
Hal Weller, Alumnus
Dr. Samuel Pellman, Alumnus
Brian Joyce, Alumnus
Dr. Clayton Parr, Music Faculty
George Beverley, Alumnus
Roger Miller, Alumnus
Andrea Ridilla, Music Faculty
John Heard, Music Faculty
Hal Grossman, Music Faculty
Eleanore Vail, Western College Faculty
Sandra Seefeld, Emerita

Appendix I

Credits

Dr. Everett F. Nelson, Chair, Dept. of Music 1951–1972
Robert Schmidt, Director, Miami University Archives
Lynn Smith-Bartram, Library Assistant, Miami University
Jacqueline Johnson, Western College Archivist
James Lentini, Dean, School of Creative Arts, 2007–2013
Barbara Wright, Department of Music, Miami University
Professor William Albin, Music Faculty
Professor Kay Edwards, Music Faculty
Professor Jack Liles, Music Faculty
Professor Jeffrey Kimball, Department of History
Frank Jordan, Professor Emeritus, Miami University
John Eicher, Professor Emeritus, Miami University
Jacqueline Kraft, Luxembourg photo archivist
Paulette Barone, Luxembourg photo archivist

PHOTOGRAPHY

Known photographers are credited beneath each photo.
Miami University Archives, Miami University Libraries, Oxford, OH
Jeff Sabo, Director, Miami University Photographic Services
Michael Tammaro

Appendix I

BIBLIOGRAPHIC SOURCES

All information concerning music faculty members was obtained from faculty records in the Miami University Archives. All historical information, including quoted material throughout this text, came from in-house publications: The Miami Student, the campus newspaper; Recensio, the Miami University yearbook; and faculty and administrative bulletins. Sources of quoted material are provided within the text. Individual faculty members contributed comments through live interviews. General historical information about the Miami University Department of Music was also gathered from the University website and from University Archive sources.

About the Author

Jerome Stanley received a PhD from the University of Cincinnati College-Conservatory of Music and is an emeritus professor from Miami University's Department of Music, where he taught for more than thirty-five years. He received a music scholarship from the Edwin B. Garrigues Foundation for undergraduate study at Washington University in St. Louis. As a young musician he won the St. Louis Symphony Young Artist Competition, which led to a debut solo recital and an appearance as concerto soloist with orchestra. He has appeared as a piano soloist, chamber musician and accompanist, performing in both Europe and the United States.

In 1983-84, while on leave from Miami University, he did post-doctoral studies in music therapy at Florida State University, Tallahassee, supported by a grant for mid-career development from the Ella Lyman Cabot Trust. He taught twice as a Visiting Scholar, in 1979 and 1997, at the Miami University Dolibois European Center in the Grand Duchy of Luxembourg, and also at that Center as a Core Professor during two years, 1987-89.

Most of his career has been devoted to teaching. He is author of a book on the life and works of British music theorist William Holder (The Edwin Mellen Press, 2002) and a book entitled *Parallels in the Arts* (Brown & Benchmark, 1995), which explores relationships between visual arts and music.

www.ingramcontent.com/pod-product-compliance
Lightning Source LLC
Chambersburg PA
CBHW022014300426
44117CB00005B/190